PUPPY TRAINING FOR BEGINNERS

THE COMPLETE GUIDE TO RAISING THE PERFECT DOG WITH CRATE TRAINING, POTTY TRAINING, AND OBEDIENCE TRAINING

BRIAN MCMILLAN

PUBLISHING FORTE

ISBN - Ebook: 978-1-954937-18-5
ISBN - Paperback: 978-1-954937-19-2
ISBN - Audiobook: 978-1-954937-20-8

INTRODUCTION

Thank you, and congratulations for purchasing the book "*Puppy Training for Beginners*."

This "Puppy Training" book contains proven steps and strategies for training and raising your pup into a happy and well-behaved dog.

Puppies can be a handful, but there's no doubt that they are man's best friend! They can lighten your life considerably, but they can also make it worse if not properly trained. This book will teach you how to handle the arrival of a new pup in the house and make sure he turns into your best friend rather than your worst enemy. By the end of this book, your puppy should know all the basic commands and fit perfectly with your now-enriched lifestyle.

We watch our puppies grow, seeing them scamper and often tumble into a clumsy heap while learning all about gravity and balance. Yet, one can't help but smile while our roly-poly fur balls fully enjoy their zest for life.

It may or may not be your first venture into the ownership of a canine companion, but even if it is your second rodeo, there may be some things you want to consider. For example, it may have been a long time since you last had a puppy, and you might need a refresher course on things like choosing the correct breed for you, stocking up on the right supplies, keeping your puppy safe, and even nutrition advice.

I want you to be prepared and know what to expect when you take on the responsibilities of a puppy. Don't misunderstand me; I love dogs and puppies, but they are a commitment, and you have to understand the puppy playbook when it comes to leash training, basic commands, crate training, and potty training.

What makes dogs so popular? They are the only creature around that will give you unconditional love and loyalty. No matter if you had a bad day at work or school or experienced a bitter disappointment, your dog will always greet you at the door, bringing tributes of bones and toys with a tail wagging as hard as possible. They give you everything they have and more.

If you are part of a family, everyone must be part of the decision. It is never fair to the dog if a family member dislikes them, ignores them, or is mean to them. Additionally, dogs will need a primary caretaker and, no matter if your kids swear that they will do it all, it is the adult that will have to make sure that there is clean water, timely feedings, daily walks, and proper care.

Puppies are available from breeders or rescues. Sometimes, through no fault of their own, a puppy will end up languishing in a shelter even if they are a pedigree or a mixed breed. The chances are good that either way, these puppies will all need the same care and training no matter their circumstance.

Along with their cuteness and playfulness, puppies will all need guidance. That's why I am writing down everything I know to ensure both you and your puppy have the best experience possible. I want you both to have the best memories and a bond that will last your puppy's lifetime.

Thanks again for purchasing this book; I hope you enjoy it!

1

TRAINING FUNDAMENTALS AND PUPPY PREP

Puppies are naturally playful, curious, and active. Those traits will be fun most of the time, but to keep your friend safe and protected, you want to help him establish boundaries. The best tip to start with is to think about your puppy like you would a human child. Treat him as if he were a toddler. Here are some puppy training principles that you can use to teach your puppy everything he needs to know to start the journey of becoming your best friend.

Show Affection

Make sure you give your puppy a lot of affection. It is effortless for you to show your puppy that you disapprove of specific behavior, but you also must show the dog a lot of affection when you are proud of his behavior. If the only thing the puppy ever receives is disapproval, he will not build a bond with you, and he will become depressed.

Communicating Your Intentions Clearly

There's nothing wrong with explicitly telling your puppy "no," only that it often fails to offer enough information. Instead, you can tell him what you want. Dogs don't usually generalize well, so if the dog jumps on someone in excitement and you say "no," he may jump higher or change direction. A better alternative would be to instruct him to sit. Telling him what you want helps avoid confusion.

One of the biggest mistakes when trying to use voice commands is to use too many words. Your dog can associate words, but it takes some time. You'll want a word that is to the point. Finish learning one command before moving on to another. If you move on to other commands too quickly, then your dog may get confused.

Be Consistent

You have to be consistent if you want your puppy to be consistent. For example, you can't work for an hour on a sit command and not take up his training again for a week or two. You have to work on the same command until he gets it right.

Establish routines with your puppy, such as regular feeding times, walk, playtimes, and bathroom breaks. Stick with your routines, and this will help speed up the process. It's not just about training commands, either. For example, a routine for your puppy will help him get up when you do, play when you feel up to it, and eat when you can feed him. This way, you aren't rearranging your schedule to take care of your puppy. Instead, you'll be teaching him to work on your schedule so that he works with you.

If you don't want your puppy to jump on people when they come through the front door, you need to reinforce that expectation every time. Allowing the pup to jump all over your sister, but not your neighbor, will confuse him. Use the "sit" or "stay" or "heel" commands to get your puppy's attention, and do it every time. Be consistent since inconsistencies will only confuse him and prolong the training process.

Be Patient

Don't allow yourself to get frustrated or impatient during the training process—either with yourself or your new puppy. It will take some time to accomplish all the goals you have set for your new pal and for you to get the hang of your puppy's unique personality, likes, and the techniques and rewards that work best for him.

Give your puppy time to understand new commands. He most likely won't learn it the first couple of times when you teach him. Repeat old commands in new training sessions so that he doesn't forget them. The attention span is pretty short, so keep your sessions frequent but short in duration; otherwise, your pup will become bored.

Never get impatient with your puppy or call him to you if you are going to punish him—all that will do is teach him that coming to you is not a good thing. Keep your voice firm but gentle, and never let any frustration creep into it.

Use Repetition

Repetition is key in dog training. For example, ask your dog to sit and give him a treat for the first two times. Then, try a different type of reward for the third time, such as petting and praise. It will teach him that he gets rewarded in different ways by listening to your commands, and this type of repetition can be extremely useful in training your puppy.

. . .

Treats and Rewards

Everyone, including puppies, loves treats. You can use these as a reward for good behavior. Dog treats come in all flavors, sizes, and specialties. Soft, meaty treats are very enticing to most puppies, and having a ready supply on hand will help your puppy quickly learn what behaviors are wanted and rewarded. Puppies usually love treats with cheese, peanut butter, or meat flavor—select small treats instead of big ones that require a lot of chewing. The trick with training is to use quick, positive reinforcement and small, bite-sized treats as a perfect reward for your puppy.

Drop a treat into the crate to lure your dog inside. Provide a treat anytime the puppy goes to the bathroom outside or sits and rolls over when commanded. Don't give your dog treats for no reason, as it will confuse the situation because he won't realize he's being rewarded.

Make sure your puppy enjoys the treats you provide. Just because a package claims that dogs like the treat does not mean your puppy will love it. If the dog doesn't enjoy the treat you give him for the behavior you expect of him, he will not be motivated to do what you say.

Your rewards should also vary. For example, if you always give him a treat following a voice command, he will associate the command with food. However, if he doesn't want or need food, then he'll refuse the command. So instead, if your rewards include giving him a treat, soothing him, playing with him, or petting him, then he knows that he will get some reward when following the command. This way, a puppy will learn to always listen to his commands.

Listen to Your Puppy

When you are training your puppy, make sure you pay attention to how the dog feels and listen to him. If the puppy doesn't cooperate, he may be trying to tell you that he needs a break, that he is not feeling well, or needs a nap. Make sure your puppy can focus on you completely. Many people find that morning time is a great time to train a dog after eating, drinking, and relieving himself.

Train Yourself

When you introduce a new dog into your household and your life, you're not just training the puppy. You're training yourself as well. Your life will have to change, and you need to be prepared for it and willing to adapt. Sleeping in until noon on the weekends is no longer an option when you have a puppy that needs to be walked and fed. Taking off for a spontaneous vacation sounds like fun, but first, you'll have to make arrangements for the pup. Working with the dog to be calm and quiet when friends and family visit takes a lot of energy and a willingness to hang in there for the long term.

You are working on forming a lifelong bond. Be patient and consistent with the process, and it will work. All the puppy training principles in the world won't work if you have a short fuse or lack interest in making your puppy comfortable and well-behaved. For specific puppy training advice, you can call on experts in the field. Pet stores, veterinarians, and fellow dog owners can all help you and your puppy become good roommates and family members.

Puppy Supplies Checklist

Bowls for Water and Food

Try to go for stainless steel ones. Plastic ones will be chewed, and you'll have to replace them every week.

. . .

Dog Crate

A dog crate is like a cage where dogs can sleep and spend time when you're out of the house. This protects your property by keeping your puppy from destroying your house while you cannot supervise him. It's also a way for your new puppy to feel safe. While there might be some whimpering and resistance the first time you confine your pup to a crate, the training will work quickly, and your dog will become accustomed to its security.

Crates come in several different sizes, and you can find crates that are metal, plastic, and even fabric. When shopping for a crate, look for crates just large enough for your puppy to stand and turn around in. If your puppy soon grows too large for a crate, look for larger crates that include a crate divider. This way, you can use the crate divider to block off half the crate until your puppy grows large enough to fill the crate space, and you avoid the expense of buying multiple crates. Put the crate in your bedroom at night if your dog has separation anxiety. Many people also find that placing an article of their clothing or an old towel inside the crate is a good idea; the dog will be comforted by your scent.

A Collar or Harness

A collar is a functional accessory that your dog will wear around his neck. The collar can attach to a leash when it's time to go for a walk, and it can also be used to hold any dog tags or documentation that you received when you registered your puppy. You should choose a light, flat collar for a puppy because your puppy is not used to having the extra weight around his neck. Go for something in soft leather or nylon. You can move on to other forms of collars after your puppy has grown up.

. . .

When you are gathering your supplies, buy items that can grow with your puppy. Collars should be adjustable and checked frequently for a proper fit. Puppies grow quickly, and you do not want the collar to be too tight or uncomfortable. When fitting your puppy's collar, be sure that you can fit two fingers between the collar and his neck. This measurement will help ensure the collar is snug enough to keep your puppy secure but won't be tight and uncomfortable. If your puppy starts to scratch at his collar, distract him with a toy, treat, or with verbal distractions to take his mind off it. When you're shopping for collars, make sure the collar you select has a sturdy metal ring to attach the leash to when you begin to leash train and walk your puppy.

There is no need to purchase a choke chain or choke collar because rewarding the positive behavior will reinforce any behavior you are trying to teach the dog.

A harness is also a great tool for puppy training, especially for small breeds and breeds with thin necks.

A Leash

The leash accompanies the collar, especially if you don't have an outdoor space where your puppy can run free. It might seem like walking on a leash should be second nature to your puppy, but it's a learned behavior.

Look for a leash that is secure and fits well on the collar or the harness you're using. When selecting the first leash to use for your puppy, pick a lightweight one. A heavy leash may add pressure to the puppy's neck and make leash training more difficult than it needs to be. Instead, give the puppy enough leash space to roam around independently, but not so much leash that the dog can run into traffic or get into trouble. Retractable leashes are often a good option because you can decide how much freedom you want to give your little buddy.

Identification Tags

Identification tags are law in many places. Have your new pup's name and your phone number added. It is best to have your puppy microchipped. If you bought your puppy from a rescue center, this might already have been done. You just need to make sure the details are changed on the register.

Chew Toys

All puppies like to chew, especially if they are teething. So it is a good idea to buy chew toys. Just make sure you buy non-toxic ones that will last and not splinter in your pup's mouth.

Grooming Equipment

Grooming isn't just about keeping their coats healthy and shiny. It's a way of bonding with your pup. You will need a comb and a brush.

Stair Gates

Stair gates and other ways of making sure certain areas are out of bounds to a pup. Ponds, stairs, balconies, and even certain rooms in the house need to be cordoned off before the puppy arrives.

Food

You must get the right food. If the puppy comes from a rescue center, try to get the same food he is already on to start with, which will help him settle in. When you change his food, do it a little at a time to not upset his delicate stomach.

Vet

Get recommendations for a good vet and get your puppy registered. As soon as he is settled, take him for a visit and a checkup.

Pet insurance. Shop around for quotes and get the right kind of pet insurance. Make sure you have the right kind of coverage and that you know the claims process.

Puppy-Proofing Your Home

One of the first things you will need to do with a new puppy is to puppy-proof your home. It is important to provide a safe environment for your puppy and make sure that it is free of hazards that may hurt your pooch somehow. In addition, puppy-proofing your home is also essential if you care about your things and don't want to find your shoes all chewed up on the floor.

Indoors

- Tiny objects that can be easily swallowed up, such as coins or rubber bands, should be kept out of reach.
- Never leave food lying around. Alcohol, chocolate, coffee, onions, and sugar can cause serious problems to your puppy's digestive system. In addition, tobacco, smoking patches, and nicotine gum can be fatal if ingested. Also, be aware that food scraps, such as chicken bones, coffee grounds, or uncooked meats can be a health hazard to your puppy.
- Puppies love to chew on electrical and cable cords, which can cause burns or electric shock. You can buy cord concealers or protective cable wrap to keep your electrical cords and your puppy safe.

• Never leave CDs or DVDs lying around. A puppy can chew them into sharp shards, which will do some serious damage.

• Everyday cleaning supplies should be kept out of the puppy's reach or behind childproof locks. Also, keep in mind that toxic vapors can get into the puppy's eyes and lungs while you are cleaning. So your puppy should be kept in another room.

• All medications and vitamins should be kept out of the puppy's reach. Never keep pills on the counter, table, or dresser. Your curious puppy can easily chew through a plastic container and happily do so if given a chance.

• Bathtubs and sinks filled with water are a potential drowning hazard. Also, keep the lid on your toilet.

• Space heaters, fireplaces, or candles should never be left on when your puppy is alone in a room, even for a minute.

• Put any sentimental or precious items out of the puppy's reach. Even if they're not toxic, you want to be sure your puppy doesn't decide some beloved old photograph is a fun chew toy.

• Some puppies mistake cat feces for food! If you have a cat, keep its litter box separated from the puppy using a baby gate.

Tip: Keep your puppy where there's flooring (tile, wood, etc.), so it will be easy for you to clean.

Outdoors

• If you have a yard, your puppy needs to be in a fenced-in area or an outdoor kennel to keep him from straying and investigating the neighborhood.

• A swimming pool is a real problem. You could put a cover over the pool until your puppy is old enough.

• Take care of the lawn regularly. Ticks can be hazardous for puppies.

• If there are toxic plants in your yard, get rid of them, as your puppy can mistake them for a snack.

- If your yard has been treated with pesticides, keep your puppy away from it.
- Be sure to block any access to a shed or garage that contains insecticide, gasoline, paint, oil, or fertilizer. Your puppy will like the taste of rat poison or antifreeze, which can be fatal.
- Clean up after your puppy and make sure he doesn't eat his waste.

Tip: Pick a place in your yard to make it the puppy's bathroom. This will instill good habits and will also save you from cleaning feces from all over the yard.

2

HOW TO CHOOSE THE RIGHT PUPPY FOR YOU

Deciding to bring a puppy into your life is a big commitment and comes with significant responsibilities. Before getting a puppy, it is important to consider if everyone in your family is ready to have one. If you find the right puppy, you will have many years of joy with a loyal companion. If the puppy is not a good fit for you or your family, there will be stress and headache ahead. Therefore, take your time and effort when looking for a puppy. Following is some advice on how to choose the right puppy for you.

Are You Ready for a Puppy?

Bringing home a puppy is one of life's most precious moments. After the initial thrill of bringing the puppy home, however, you'll need to be aware of the responsibility and commitment required to look after your new canine family member properly. Following are some questions to answer when deciding whether the time is right for a puppy in your household.

. . .

• Do you have time to train your puppy and give him the attention he needs?

Just like a child, a puppy needs a lot of time and patience when he is young. You'll need to be prepared to invest many hours into toilet training, socialization with humans and other animals, training him in behavior in your house, and establishing off-limits items. Training your puppy will ensure he grows to be a well-behaved and obedient dog but is a process that continues throughout your dog's lifetime. Your new puppy will demand attention; should you neglect him, he can become bored, leading to destructive behavior.

• Do you lead an active lifestyle?

As well as training, puppies need a lot of attention and require plenty of activity. You need to ask yourself whether you can commit to this even on those days when the weather is bad, or you're tired. Playing with a puppy helps him to burn energy and maintain his health. Taking your puppy out for walks will also expose him to other people, sights, smells, and loud noises. While some dog breeds are more energetic than others, all dogs need adequate exercise, and you must be prepared to commit to a daily exercise regime. This can be easier if you have energetic children and have more time to spend with the puppy.

• Have you considered the costs of owning a puppy?

It would be best if you were sure that you could take on the financial responsibilities of owning a dog. These costs can range from food and toys to visits to a veterinarian for spaying or neutering, vaccines, and other needs. You may also want to invest in professional training to ensure that your dog is well-behaved. People tend to forget that dogs incur expenses during puppyhood and throughout their lives. An unexpected veterinarian bill in case of injury or other emergencies can be very expensive; some people buy pet insurance to offset potentially high veterinary costs.

Should You Get a Purebred or Mixed-Breed Puppy?

Deciding on what breed of puppy you want is also an important decision. With a purebred puppy, you'll know his parents (and other ancestors) are all the same breed, and the puppy will conform to the specific characteristics of that breed. In addition, with a purebred puppy, you'll have a good indication of his general physical and behavioral characteristics, as well as how big he'll get.

You can obtain purebred dogs from responsible breeders, but they will likely be more expensive than a mixed-breed puppy. You should also check with shelters since many also have purebred dogs available.

All breeds are different, so be sure to do your research first. You have to consider young children or whether you are planning a family at some stage—not all breeds are suitable for young children.

While a mixed-breed dog will have a more diverse genetic makeup than a purebred, most mixed-breed dogs' appearance, size, and nature can still be predicted (since they result from both dog breeds' characteristics). For example, if both parents are small, the puppy will grow up to be a small dog. The same goes if the parents are large, but you will not know if you have mixed-size parents.

. . .

Purebred dogs are more prone to hereditary conditions such as arthritis. Be sure to check out the parents and do your homework on the breed you are considering. Look for breed-specific behaviors. These genetic behaviors are inherited and will most certainly have some effect on your puppy when he grows up.

It shouldn't matter whether you want a purebred or a mixed breed because, if you get your pup at the right age, most behavioral traits can be trained out of him.

Should You Choose a Large or Small Breed, Male or Female?

When choosing the breed of your puppy, you'll need to consider whether you want a large or small dog; space considerations may be a factor, for example, as well as the extra care a large dog can require. Also, remember that if you choose a medium, large, or giant breed with the general characteristics of medium or high aggression toward people or other dogs, you'll need to take this into account in their training and handling.

Female dogs tend to be smaller, less aggressive, and easier to train, whereas male dogs tend to be more affectionate. Male dogs are often more playful, making it relatively harder to keep them focused during training.

Buying a Puppy from Private Sales

When you look for a puppy, try to avoid pet shops. Most dogs at pet stores come from puppy mills.

You will find plenty of advertisements for puppies on websites, in the local newspapers, or pinned on bulletin boards in your local shops. Some will be free to good homes. After you have decided whether you want a purebred or mixed breed, you can start narrowing the ads down.

If you find an ad that interests you and you are not an expert on dogs or have never had one before, it is a good idea to bring someone along who has experience.

Always make sure you see the puppy in its home environment with its mother. This is vital, as it's the first clue that the puppy is coming from a happy, healthy home.

Adopting from a Shelter

Animal shelters are full of dogs and puppies that need homes, and some shelters also specialize in certain breeds. Although most are adult dogs, you will find puppies at shelters, and you can be assured that, provided it's a reputable and fully licensed shelter, they will have been looked after well. You can adopt a puppy for a fraction of the cost compared to buying at a pet store or breeder. For a puppy that you rescue from a shelter, the following costs are normally covered: spaying or neutering, vaccinations, test for heart-worm, flea and tick treatments, and microchip.

Adopting from a shelter means you probably will not get to see the parents. Also, bear in mind that your puppy will behave differently in your home from what you see in the shelter.

Shelter dogs require a lot of extra care and attention. Some of them may have been mistreated (even puppies), and they will need a lot of love and attention to help them learn to trust again. Not all shelter dogs are in this situation, though. Some of them have come from loving homes, from people who simply couldn't give them the time they needed.

Buying from a Breeder

Buying from a breeder is another option to find an ideal puppy, although not all breeders are reputable. If you have your heart set on a purebred, contact your local Kennel Club or the association for the breed you are looking for.

When you visit a breeder, take a good look around the premises. Are they clean and well-kept? What are the older dogs like? Are they happy, healthy, and friendly?

Ask if the breeder has a waiting list. Good breeders are popular, and if they have a waiting list, then it's a good sign. Find out if the puppies are raised with lots of human interaction right from the start. This shows that the important process of socialization has begun, along with some of the house and obedience training.

Have a good look at the puppy's parents; a proper breeder will have both parents ready to show you. Ask as many questions as you feel are necessary. Again, a good breeder will answer all of your questions without holding back. You may want to know if they are willing to accept the puppy back if things don't go as planned.

If you choose to buy from a specific breeder, they should give you all the information you need on health care advice, such as vaccinations, worming, etc., their feeding schedule, and some will even offer future support if needed.

Things to Look for When Deciding on a Puppy

Once you've decided what breed of puppy you want, you'll need to choose one from a litter. Following are some things to keep in mind when making your choice.

• Your puppy should be no younger than eight weeks as this is the optimum time when they should have been weaned from their mother.

• If you have decided on a specific breed, see if you can find people who have adult dogs of the breed and get to know them. Go to shows, clubs, and ask questions. You will also get an idea of the eventual size of your pup. In addition, vets are good people to speak to, as they may be able to provide you with information regarding specific breeds—in particular, about any inherent problems.

• Talk to the owner and ask about the pups' general health, whether they are eating well, and if they're regularly eliminating. Check whether they have been tested for parasites and have been dewormed—this needs to occur every two weeks, starting from when they are two weeks old. Also, ask whether you can see the puppies' parents to get an idea of their characteristics, which are likely hereditary.

• Observe the puppy in his litter. In any litter, some pups will be more assertive while others hang back and are quieter. Look for confidence in a pup but not one that is so confident he knocks the others out of the way! Try to avoid shy pups or those who are scared. No puppy of that age should show any of this, so that could indicate a problem. You may also find that less assertive pups and more aggressive pups behave differently when not in a group.

• Check their energy levels and overall appearance. As stated in the previous point, the amount of energy and assertiveness you want your puppy to have is up to you, but puppies should be full of energy and playful in general. While they tend to be clumsy when small, make sure that they don't have a limp and can support their weight evenly across their four legs. Their coats should have a healthy shine, there should be no dull or flaky areas visible, and there should be no bald spots, sores, or redness on their skin.

Making Your Choice

Once you've assessed the litter as a whole and narrowed down your choices to one or two pups, you should examine them more closely and pay attention to:

- **Any obvious signs of illness or injury.** A good pup should be well-rounded—neither fat nor skinny.
- **Eyes** – They should be clear with no redness or hair loss around them.
- **Ears** – There should be no discharge and the ear flaps covered in healthy hair; puppies constantly scratching their ears may be a sign of problems.
- **Head** – The top of a puppy's head often has a small soft spot. If this area is larger than a small coin, it may indicate future issues called "open fontanels."
- **Nose** – There can be some clear discharge from the nose, but if it is colored, this is an issue. The puppy should be able to breathe easily without any noise through their nose.
- **Mouth** – A puppy's gums should be moist and have a healthy pink color; their bottom and top sets of teeth should align unless they have a breed-specific underbite (such as bulldogs, for example).

When you have narrowed down your choices, it's time to do a little hearing test. Have the puppy facing away from you or playing with another dog or person, and then stamp your foot or drop your keys on the floor. The puppy's reaction should be immediate. They may be slightly startled at the noise but should come over to see what all the fuss is about—not run and hide. This will not only weed out dogs that may be frightened of their shadow but also determine if they are deaf.

. . .

When you think you have made a choice, pick the puppy up. Cuddle him (not too hard, of course!) and see what his reactions are. If he struggles and won't settle down, this may not be the pup for you. Most puppies will struggle a little and will then settle and examine you.

Touch the puppy all over its body, including the mouth, ears, and paws. Any pup who has been properly handled will not shy away from this.

Ask to see the veterinary records for the pup and check vaccination dates. And, if possible, get a reputable vet to check your pup over before you decide to take him home.

Puppies are adorable, but they're also a lot of work. Before you take the plunge into new puppy ownership, make sure you're willing to invest the time, emotional energy, and resources.

3

HOUSE-TRAINING YOUR PUPPY

House-training your pup will require you to exercise a lot of patience, consistency and be fully committed. You should also understand that accidents must happen. However, when you follow the instructions below carefully, your new family member will be well trained in just a few weeks.

NOTE: It can take up to one year for your pup to be fully trained without accidents happening. To start house-training your pup, the puppy needs to be at least 12 weeks or older. At this age, the bladders of puppies are usually well-formed to hold urine.

Potty Training

For many people, potty training their puppy is the most daunting part of bringing a new puppy into the family. One of the biggest reasons puppies and dogs end up in shelters is that they have not successfully trained them. Potty training a puppy can be time-consuming and messy. However, it's essential for your dog's growth and development, as well as your peace of mind.

. . .

WAIT Until Your Puppy Is the Right Age

Puppies younger than twelve to sixteen weeks old simply do not have enough control over their bladders to be potty trained. Hold off on potty training until your puppy is at least twelve weeks old. Until then, keep a supply of disposable or washable puppy pads your puppy can use. These pads usually have a scent embedded in them that attracts the puppy to eliminate them. If you see your puppy using the bathroom off the pad, gently pick him up, move him to the pad, and praise him for using the potty.

CREATING a Routine

Once your puppy has reached the right age, it's important to establish a potty training routine and to be consistent and patient with it. The first step is to create a schedule. Puppies and dogs do best when they follow a routine. Having a schedule teaches the dog that there are specific times for him to do specific activities. For example, there is a specific time for him to eat, there is a specific time each day for him to go for a walk, and there are specific times each day for him to be taken outside to relieve himself.

MOST PUPPIES CAN HOLD their bladder for one hour every month of their age. This means that he can hold his bladder for three hours if the puppy is three months old. However, it would be best if you never make him hold it for any amount of time longer than that.

BEGIN by taking your puppy outside at least every two hours. You will also want to take the puppy outside as soon as he wakes up in the morning, before bed at night, after playtime, as well as after he has had something to eat or drink.

. . .

It is also important to watch for bathroom "tells" puppies often display. Twirling in circles, whining, scratching, and sniffing the floor are often indications the puppy needs to potty, so if you see or hear these things, take him outside immediately.

It is important to pick a place outside for your dog's bathroom area. This is because you do not want the dog going all over the yard, and you want to build a routine with him. Take your puppy to the same spot every time to use the bathroom. He will be able to sniff the area and know where he went to the bathroom before. Be patient with your puppy; do not try to force him, yell at him, or rush him to use the potty. Simply stand in the designated spot and use upbeat, positive verbal encouragements to "go potty" and allow your puppy time to sniff out the perfect spot and relieve himself.

Once your puppy does his business, be sure to reward him with positive praise, a lot of snuggles, pets, and kisses. You can give your puppy a treat after he has relieved himself outside, but remember to do this while you are still outside and not when you have gone back into the house. Make potty training a rewarding, happy experience, so your dog feels good when he sees you get the leash and say the words "go potty." Most puppies truly want to please their masters, and letting your puppy know he is good and did the right thing will help your puppy's potty training progress at a faster rate.

Regular Feeding

The next step is to make sure you feed your puppy on a regular schedule. Depending on the puppy's age, he will need to eat between three and four times a day. If you feed your puppy on a schedule, it is more likely he will need to relieve himself at the same time each day, which will make house training much easier for both of you. Your puppy's digestive system is quick and efficient, and taking him out fifteen minutes after he eats will help get him used to go potty outside.

You should also make sure you pick up the puppy's food and water bowl at least two and a half hours before going to bed. This will help ensure the puppy does not eat too close to bedtime or in the middle of the night, which will help ensure the puppy does not relieve himself in the house while everyone is asleep.

Puppies cannot be expected to hold their bladders all night, so you will also need to set the alarm during the night so you can take him outside once or twice the first couple of weeks. Expecting your puppy to hold his bladder throughout the night is not only unrealistic; it is a surefire way to ensure he soils his crate or gets a bladder infection trying to hold it for longer than he is capable of.

The puppy may wake up in the middle of the night and need to relieve himself. Remain as quiet and calm as possible if this happens. First, do not turn on all of the lights in the house, but turn on as few as you can. Next, do not talk to the puppy or pet him. Simply take him out, tell him to go potty, reward him when he is finished, and bring him back inside. If you talk to him, he will likely think it is time to get up and play, which means he will not go back to sleep when you return indoors.

Preventing Accidents

It is important to keep an eye on the puppy when you are potty training him. Do not allow him to have access to the entire house because this will raise the chance of him soiling in a hidden area when he's out of your line of sight. Keep doors to bedrooms closed, and use dog gates to keep your pup within your line of vision at all times.

When you can't watch your puppy, it's a good idea to leave him in a crate or on a leash.

It's important to remember that even the smartest puppies don't have bladder control yet. Young dogs also don't know how to tell you when they need to eliminate their waste. They may be aware of it, but they have not yet figured out how to tell you.

If He Doesn't Listen

If your dog doesn't listen, then you need to provide more training. Pay attention to what he likes. Does he like praise more than treats? Are you making sure to vary it? You should have started with treats and progressed to praise. Also, you could be trying to rush your puppy. If you rush him, he won't go to the right area because he feels the need to hurry. Puppies can pick up on your impatience, so try to calm down.

How to Crate Train Your Dog

Although crate training your pup may require you to invest your time and effort, it's worth it. You can use the crate in a wide range of scenarios, including limiting his access to the rest of the house, creating a safe space for him, or transporting him.

To prepare, you should start by selecting a proper crate, as advised earlier in the book. It would be best if you also kept in mind that the whole process might go for a few days or weeks, requiring exercise patience.

. . .

Step 1: Introducing your pup to the crate

Position the crate in one area of the house, preferably where your family spends most of their time (maybe the family room). Lay a towel or soft blanket inside the crate. Bring your pup over to the crate and talk to him in a happy tone.

To encourage the puppy to get inside the crate, drop a couple of tiny treats near it. Once he finishes those, drop a couple more inside the door, then when he is done, drop more treats at the back of the crate. If he does not want to go in and get the treats at the far end of the crate, do not force him.

If he is not motivated by the treats, you can try tossing his favorite toy into the crate. Repeat this step until he is comfortable getting inside (it might take a few days). Do not close the door on him in this step.

Step 2: Feeding the pup his meals inside the crate

Once the puppy is comfortable getting into the crate, you should start feeding him all the meals near the crate. Doing this will create a positive association with the crate.

If he enters the crate readily, put his food dish to the far end of the crate. However, if he looks anxious or reluctant to get in, put the dish in only as far as he is willing to go and extend the distance as he becomes comfortable.

Step 3: Start closing the door

Once the pup can stand comfortably in the crate and eat his meal, you can now close the door as he eats. Open the door immediately, he finishes eating. With more meals, leave the door closed for a few more minutes until he stays for about 10 minutes inside the crate after eating. If he starts crying or whining, you should not let him out, as this teaches him that the only way to get out of the crate is to whine. Wait until he stops to let him out.

Step 4: Leave him inside for longer

Once your pup is completely comfortable taking his meals inside the crate, you should start confining him without mealtime. You can start by calling him over the crate and giving him a treat. Throw a treat inside and praise him when he gets in, then close the door. Sit near the crate for 5-10 minutes, then go into another room for a few more minutes. Come back to the crate and sit there for a few more minutes. Once done, let him out of the crate. Repeat this step a couple of times per day. With each repetition, increase the time you leave your pup in the crate and the time you are out of the room.

Once he can stay in the crate without crying or whining for around 30 minutes when you are out of his sight, then you can begin leaving him in the crate when you are out for short periods. You can also let him sleep inside the crate at night.

Paper training

The paper-training method is where you use newspapers and encourage your puppy to use these for going to the bathroom. You can also use special 'wee wee' pads scented with a chemical that attracts the puppy to use them. You can get these at any local pet store. They can make training easier, but they can be more costly as well. If you intend to continue using the pads, make sure you start with them and not paper. Don't mix newspaper and pads, or your results will be very inconsistent.

. . .

THE FIRST THING you want to do is choose a confinement area, either in a very small room or a room you can enclose with baby gates. Most people choose a bathroom, laundry room, or kitchen area because these rooms are usually covered in tile or other floorings easy to keep clean. The confinement area should only be big enough for your pup's bed, food and water bowls, and his designated potty area.

THERE SHOULD BE no visible floor space in the confinement area. The floor should have the bed or crate in one section, and newspapers or pads should cover the rest of the space. Using a small area, you are encouraging your pup to use the covered area of the floor to relieve himself. This will get him used to do his business on the newspapers or pads.

WHEN HE DOES soil on the newspapers, try to clean them up as quickly as possible. You may want to consider leaving a rag that has a little of his urine on it in the designated spot to help him recognize where he's supposed to go if you're using a newspaper. The pads are already scented to attract the puppy to go there. There are also house-training sprays you can buy at any big pet store that serve the same purpose. The pheromones in them attract the puppy back to the right spot. These sprays can also be used outdoors if you want to direct him to a certain area.

ONCE YOUR PUP becomes accustomed to potting on the newspapers, you can make the covered area smaller. You should have noticed which section of the area he has used most often and keep all that section well covered. Next, start uncovering the area very close to his crate/bed and bowls.

. . .

THE GOAL IS to continuously limit the designated 'inside potty area' by making the papered area smaller and smaller while giving him frequent access to his 'outdoor potty area. Therefore you must spend as much time as possible with your puppy so you can get him to his outdoor area as often as possible.

THE KEY to quick and successful housebreaking using the paper training method depends on how much supervised training you spend with your pup. The more times you can get him outside to do his business and reward him, the quicker he will learn.

Litter Pan Training

Litter pan training is growing in popularity. Many dogs take to it very well, and it provides an easier, cleaner indoor option than just a space on the kitchen floor. For dog owners living in high-rise buildings, people with limited mobility, or unsuited dogs for the weather where they live, pan training allows ease and comfort for both owners and dogs.

A DOG TRAINED to a litter pan will still potty outdoors when going 'walkies,' but he has another option as well. Since little dogs need to go more often than their bigger cousins, it's very helpful for them to have a good indoor area to relieve themselves while their owners are away from home. Eight hours for a large dog is like 'holding it' for 24 hours to a little guy! Not a very reasonable expectation.

IF A LITTER PAN of some type is your chosen route, make sure you have it ready to go before beginning house training. Find a convenient spot in your home to place it, and don't move it around except when you need to set up a confinement area. Your puppy needs to learn where to find it! You can relocate it once he's trained.

. . .

IF YOUR DOG is not a toy breed, you'll need to provide a larger pan as he grows. Many people start with a traditional dog litter pan and change to a round one since dogs like to circle before pooping. For a larger dog, this could even be something like a 'kiddie pool,' perhaps moved into the garage or basement after he's trained.

MAKE sure that your dog can easily enter the pan without climbing or jumping. It needs to be simple for him to get in and out! You may need to cut the entryway down a bit lower so that he can step in. Some people like the pellets that are sold as litter, and there are several different types, and others use a piddle pad in the pen.

IF YOUR PUP doesn't seem to like it or tries to eat it, change to a different type of absorbing medium. [Cat litter doesn't work very well for most dogs because it gets stuck in their feet.] The fake grass models have a tray underneath which collects the urine, but many folks like to line that with wee-wee pads for quicker, easier cleaning.

BE AWARE, if you're not already, that although young male pups squat, as he matures he'll lift his leg to urinate. By that time, you need to make provisions to pee over the top of the pan or onto the wall. You can purchase posts or little plastic fire hydrants scented with attractant to give him something to aim at or use a pan with higher sides. If you have multiple dogs, you may need multiple pans. They sometimes don't want to share and won't use a pan that's already been soiled.

TO TRAIN your pup to a litter pan, **follow the same procedures as crate training.** You just take the pup to the litter pan instead of taking him outside to the yard. If you need to be away for a while, set up a confinement area with the litter pan inside, just as you would do with paper training. Be sure to cover the rest of the floor with paper (in case of accidents) until your pup is reliable with the pan!

JUST AS WITH NEWSPAPER, pads, and even the yard, the litter pan should be kept as clean as possible. Clean up messes as soon as possible, and change the litter following the instructions that come with it. Next, empty the pan for a thorough cleansing with a disinfectant cleaner at least once a week, and hose off the plastic turf as well.

Crazy Training Plan

If you would like to streamline the housebreaking process, and you can completely free yourself from any other responsibilities, work, or family for a couple of days, then this 'extreme' method might be just the thing for you. It's very effective and creates a strong bond, but it does take its toll on you. So if you're a bit of a risk-taker, read on.

THE 'CRAZY' way to house-train your pup, within his physical bladder limits, of course, is to be **completely proactive.** The pup ***never*** goes on the floor, not once. How do you achieve this miracle, you ask? With self-sacrifice and a total focus on the task, allowing no distractions. It's just you, puppy, and housebreaking.

THIS WILL WORK with a litter pan or a pad as well as going outdoors. It's a simple procedure, a sort of 'extreme crate training,' but you have to 'suck it up and follow-through—that's the craziness. It's 24/7 on your part until you reach his physical limits. After that, you never ask him to exceed those limits.

. . .

STILL WITH ME? Then here's how it goes. You bring he puppy home and let him potty before you bring him inside. Ten minutes later, you take him out again (or take him to the pan or pad). Praise a successful trip! If he doesn't go, give him another ten minutes and then out again. After each successful potty break, you add five minutes to the time between trips, so you'd wait 15 minutes and then go out again. After each unsuccessful trip, repeat the same interval.

YOU NEED to continue this all day and all night, following and adjusting the schedule. Wake up (use an alarm), wake him up (really), and go out. Work some playtime in between some of the trips, and don't forget to wedge in some food for both you and the pup. Watch some TV together. But keep track of the time! You'll become a little zombie-like, but that's OK. Think of it as a short-term extreme sporting event. Stay focused on your mission!

A THREE-MONTH-OLD PUP will settle into a 3-4 hour maximum interval between trips. Once you know what the limit is for your pup, you can make arrangements to let him relieve himself within that interval. You can also crate him and crawl into bed until your next puppy potty break (set the alarm!).

ALTHOUGH YOU'LL NEED about a day to fully recover, depending on what time of day you brought him home and started the process, you'll also have a very accurate idea of his bathroom habits and needs. In addition, you will have learned his potty rituals—does he sniff or circle, or both? (This can help you prevent future 'accidents' if he needs to go earlier than usual for some reason.)

YOU'VE EARNED HIS TRUST, and he can count on you to meet, even anticipate his needs. Of course, he's never eliminated anywhere except where you, his pack leader, have approved, so he won't be inclined to start. But, even young as he is, he'll come to you for a potty break. And, despite the sleep disruption, it is time spent working together that can give you a very strong bond with your dog. Packs work cooperatively for the good of all, and that's what you two have just done together!

THE FOLLOW-UP IS SIMPLY ASSURING that you never expect him or force him to exceed his capabilities. You get him to his designated area within his time limit, period. If you can't be there to do it, then you find someone who can help you out. This means at night, too! Set the alarm, take him for his potty break, praise him, and go back to bed. Once he's six months old or so and has full control of himself, he'll be **extremely** reliable (and sleeping through the night).

How to Handle Accidents

Accidents are going to happen. Sometimes when a young puppy gets excited, he can accidentally use the bathroom without meaning to. Just accept accidents as part of the process and do not overreact to them. Your puppy is not willful, disobedient, or resistant. It's simply part of the process, so do not punish him by spanking him, rubbing his nose in it, or yelling at him. If you notice your pup is beginning to pee or poop in the house, clap your hands or make a loud noise. You want to startle the puppy and get its attention, but you don't want to scare him. Calmly say "No" and take him to his spot outside.

WHEN AN ACCIDENT DOES OCCUR in the house, simply clean it up and move on. You cannot apply a correction after the fact that the puppy will have no idea what is going on and why he is being told "No" or what he was supposed to do. Unlike us, puppies live in the moment, and once it has passed, they do not have a recollection of the accident, so trying to discipline a puppy for a past action will only make him scared and make it difficult for him to trust you. Never, ever strike your puppy when you find accidents or for any other reason. Hitting your puppy will only crush his spirit and break the bond you are trying to build; it will not correct his behavior or make the process faster.

If the pup keeps going back to the same spot he had soiled previously, then it is possible that you are not cleaning the place well enough, or you are using a product that is not effective. Therefore, when selecting the product to use for cleaning up messes, you should:

Avoid ammonia-based products: If you use an ammonia-based product to deal with a mess, then you end up amplifying the 'bathroom smell.' For example, Pee has ammonia and so cleaning up puppy pee using an ammonia-based product will only trigger your pup to potty on the same spot.

Use Enzyme-based products: Enzyme-based cleaning products are the best choice to clean up messes. Such products contain enzymes that 'eat' the bacteria that cause the odor, eliminating the smell.

Block off access to the spots: If you do not have an enzyme-based cleaner to deal with the mess, then you can block access to the spot where your pup keeps on eliminating. You can achieve this by placing a large object on top of that spot or making a barrier around it.

Be patient and consistent with your potty training routine and be gentle, kind, and loving with your puppy. You'd never yell at, punish or scold a baby for accidents, so don't do it to your puppy. Instead, follow these potty training tips, and in just a few weeks, your puppy will be potty trained, and you can feel good about a job well done.

4

DIET AND NUTRITION

What should you give your pup to eat? How much should your puppy eat? What to use as a treat? These are all questions that new dog owners are most likely to ask themselves when thinking about adopting a puppy and training it to become an obedient adult dog.

WALKING down the food dog aisle only makes things more complicated. Unlike back in the day when there were one or two types of dog food, today's choices are pretty endless. But that's a good thing. Specialized dieting formulas and high-quality foods with essential sourcing contribute to the overall health of your puppy.

BUT, despite the apparent reason, you should choose quality ingredients for your pup – providing your puppy with a balanced diet rich in essential nutrients-something else can benefit from balanced meals besides your puppy's health, and that is its training success.

. . .

Many dog owners overlook the importance that the food has over the process of training, but the truth is, even the most straightforward directions can take a lot of time to teach if your pup is under or overfed.

Your pup will be the happiest if it has a predictable feeding routine, so make sure to provide that. Besides the fact that it thrives when a consistent schedule has been set, the regular feeding times can also support the house training process. In addition, knowing exactly when and how much your pup has eaten makes it a lot easier for you to determine its potty needs, which can be a lifesaver when training your puppy to accept his drop zone.

Understanding the Labels on Dog Food

To know whether your puppy is getting the right nutrition, you must read the label on the dog food. The first ingredient that MUST be on the label should be a specific meat. This meat can be chicken, beef, fish, or whatever, but it needs to be the real thing. If you see chicken by-products or something else right beside the meat, this means the meat is not real, and your puppy will not get the great benefits out of it. Likewise, if another ingredient is placed first, such as bone meal, meat by-product, or corn, you should stay away from this kind of food because it is unsuitable for the puppy.

So why should you pick out real meat rather than meat by-product? Aren't they the same thing? By-products are the leftovers of the meat, such as the feet, feathers, skin, hooves, and eyes. They are not suitable for dogs to eat, and you should pick out another kind of food to keep your puppy healthy. In addition, if words like meat and animal are put in place of specific products like beef or chicken, run away and pick out another product.

. . .

Now that we know the importance of getting real meat in your dog food let's look at how the labeling works. When looking at the label, the very first ingredient is the one that is found in the highest concentration in the food. The other ingredients may be added in more for flavoring or to add in some more nutrition, but by weight, the first ingredient will take up the most room out of all the ingredients.

Make sure that you get dog food that doesn't have corn in it at all. Grains and corn are not good for your puppy and have been linked with bloating joint swelling and skin allergies in many dogs. However, if you don't have a choice, make sure that corn is listed as far down on the label as possible. Also, try to keep your dog on a grain-free diet as much as possible. They are meant to enjoy meat all the time, and grains and corn can make them very sick and don't provide the right kind of nutrition that your puppy needs.

What to Feed and How Much?

Once you have chosen the perfect dog food for your puppy, you are probably curious about how much you need to feed the puppy. Of course, you want to make sure that they are well fed and not going hungry, but on the other hand, you don't want them to gain too much weight and have all those health issues. So here are some basics that you can keep in mind regarding how much to feed your puppy.

First 8 Weeks

During the first 8 weeks, the puppy should be kept with their mother. If the puppy is removed from their mother too early, they will have a lot of trouble adjusting to their new home and may cause some more issues. They are also more likely to have an increased risk of illnesses. During this time, the puppy will get some good milk from their mother, full of nutrition, and lots of antibodies to keep the puppies healthy.

. . .

Around three to four weeks, the puppy can be introduced to some solid foods but will still have some of the mother's milk. You can mix one part of the puppy milk with three parts o the food to help make it softer while the puppy gets used to the food. You will slowly keep doing this until the puppy can eat the food without having it watered down.

6 to 8 Weeks

During this time, the puppy will need to be fed 3 to 4 times each day. The puppy is going to have nutritional needs that are different from the adult dog. Make sure that you are going with puppy food rather than the adult version so that the puppy is getting the right amount of nutrition. Once the puppy reaches 8 weeks, you can probably move them down to just 2 feedings a day.

3 Months to 6 Months

This is the time when your puppy will begin to teeth. During this time, they may lose their appetite or become pickier about what they will like to eat. Keep offering up nutritious food at both of the feedings. If the puppy is dealing with a stomach upset for more than two days, you should take them in to see the vet.

6 Months to 1 Year

Even though the puppy will look like they are all grown, you need to remember that they are still considered a puppy. Therefore, make sure to continue feeding them puppy food to give them the right kind of nutrition. You can discuss with your vet when is a good time to switch the puppy off the puppy food and over to adult food, so they continue to get the right nutrition at all stages. In this stage and all the others, you will only feed the puppy about two times a day unless directed otherwise by your vet.

. . .

As the puppy gets to their adult life, you will change over the food to an adult type. This will provide the now grown-up puppy with the right nutrition to stay healthy and strong. If any health concerns come up, your vet may ask you to switch to a special kind of dog food. But if you are taking care of the puppy the way you should, regular dog food will work out just fine.

Treats

Treats are the most important factor in the process of positive training. Without these tasty rewards, your pup will not be encouraged to participate in the sessions and go through all the trouble of getting your directions right.

But, what exactly is a treat? Should you pay tons of money for the most expensive smelly bones just for the sake of luring your pup to show a shred of interest in the training? Of course, not. The treat can be pretty much anything your puppy loves to eat, even regular dog food. Most dog trainers suggest that the treat should be a mixture of regular food and more special pieces of treats.

The most important thing is for the treats to be:

- Chewy
- Rich in Aroma and Flavor
- Easy to Break
- Soft

Start with a small number of treats and mix them up with doggy food. As the training progresses, increase the treats gradually. Also, make sure to use different treats on a weekly basis, so that your pup doesn't lose interest for cooperating. Treats can be pretty much anything your puppy enjoys – from special bone-shaped doggy treats, to small pieces of cheese or sausage.

Should You Cook for Your Dog?

Some people choose to cook for their dogs, and there can be pros and cons to this choice. There are some things to consider while constructing your dog's meals:

- Are you capable of making sure that your dog receives consistent dietary requirements?
- Do you feel confident that you can manipulate the ingredients to provide the same guaranteed nutrition every day?
- Are you sure that every ingredient is dog-friendly?

THESE ARE some very important questions to consider, and studying nutritional needs can be tricky. Here are some additional things to consider:

Cons

- Are the recipes you are using safe?
- Are your ingredients safe?
- Cooking complete meals takes a considerable amount of time and labor.
- Nutritional deficiencies can cause health problems.
- Is your dog receiving their daily requirements of necessary vitamins and minerals?
- Is the diet truly well-balanced?

Pros

- You can satisfy the picky eater.
- You will be able to address concerns about food allergies.
- You can spend more time in the kitchen if you love to cook.

- You won't have to worry about food recalls
- You may enjoy cooking for your pet.

SHOULD you decide that cooking for your pet is your true calling, consult with a certified veterinary nutritionist and do not rely on recipes from the internet. If you want a custom diet designed specifically for your dog, it should be under the guidance of a specialist.

THERE ARE MORE Choices

THERE ARE a few more choices to consider:

- The raw diet consists of a mixture of organ meats, muscle meats, raw eggs, ground or whole bone, some fruits and vegetables, and a dairy product. There are owners out there that swear by the raw diet, and it can be homemade, freeze-dried, store-bought, or dehydrated. Owners should be careful when handling raw food. Many veterinarians will caution owners with young children or a family member with a compromised immune system to avoid the raw diet. You should be aware that dogs suffering from pancreatitis, cancer, and several other diseases *require* cooked food. Puppies should also have cooked food to avoid contracting parasites.

- ADDING fresh food to your kibble can end up satisfying that picky eater while still getting your dog their guaranteed analysis. Remember that our table scraps may not be suitable to add to your pup's dinner, but there are healthy alternatives. Should you want to add a little freeze-dried food, you can purchase a product called meal mixers. Even a few commercial dog foods on the market have begun to offer this alternative in their nutrition line.

. . .

If you want to have some fun with your dog's food, here are a few alternatives you could add:

- Cheese is high in protein and, as long as your dog isn't lactose intolerant, you may want to add a small dollop of cottage cheese or shredded cheddar to your dog's meal. If your dog is a bit overweight, you can use the lower-fat options.

- Adding a tablespoon of yogurt to their food is a great alternative, but you must be diligent about checking for dangerous ingredients. Some yogurt contains ingredients like xylitol, which is a human sweetener that is very dangerous to dogs. You should never give your dog sugar-free yogurt. Play it safe and stick to plain, non-fat yogurt with no fruit, artificial sweeteners, or sugar. Greek yogurt is okay as long as you check the ingredients.

- Pumpkin is THE go-to product when your dog has an upset stomach or loose stool. Make sure that you are using the plain canned pumpkin and not the pie version that contains sugar. Pumpkin is a fantastic source of vitamins A, E, and C. If you think your dog may be ill, always speak with your vet. Puppy diarrhea should always raise a red flag and should be relayed to your vet right away.

- While you are cooking yourself some breakfast, consider adding another egg to the mix and give your pup a treat. Eggs are a great source of quality protein and are always easy on the digestive system.

- Apple slices are a fun thing to share with your dog. They are a great source of fiber and can add vitamins A and C. Cut the apple up into small pieces so your dog will not risk choking. Never give your dog apple seeds because they contain cyanide and are toxic.

- PEANUT BUTTER has raised some concerns lately because some brands use xylitol in their recipes. Always double-check your labels! Regular peanut butter can be a special treat to help your dog take medications or entertain them when stuffed into a favorite toy like Kongs® or a chew toy (Kongs should never be given unsupervised).

- OATMEAL IS a great carbohydrate alternative. Just stick to the non-sweetened version and make sure there are no sugar substitutes. Of course, you can always mix this up with a bit of honey or peanut butter.

- EXTRA PROTEIN can be added in the form of fresh meat. Chicken, turkey, venison, and beef are all options that your dog will eat enthusiastically.

- FRUITS and vegetables can add a bit of fiber to your dog's diet and help fill them up without all the calories. Safe choices include green beans, sweet potatoes, squash, bananas, and blueberries.

- SALMON OIL has been known to remedy dry, itchy skin, nails that crack easily or add a little extra fat to boost calories for a dog that struggles to keep on weight. Provided your dog doesn't have an allergy to fish, this is a quality additive to your dog's diet.

Things You Should Avoid Feeding

I have gone into great detail about what is good for your puppy, but you should also be aware of food hazards. It can be tempting if your pup is staring you down with their soulful brown eyes just to give them a tiny piece of what you are eating, but there are some things that a dog should never ingest because it can cause dangerous consequences. Here is my list of foods not to provide under any circumstances:

- Avocados contain a fungal toxin known as persin. Too much of this can cause your dog to vomit or experience diarrhea. Persin can be found in avocado leaves, trees, and bark as well, so if you are thinking about growing an avocado crop, it might be best if you plant it outside your dog's area.

- Alcohol is always a bad idea when it comes to your pup. It's hard to imagine that anyone would think that this is a good idea. Just a small amount of beer, liquor, wine, or food containing alcohol can cause diarrhea, coma, vomiting, breathing problems, or death—the smaller the dog, the worse the consequences.

- Cat food is not fatal, but it is built for the digestion of cats, not dogs. Each species has different dietary requirements, and cat food can cause your dog to have nutritional imbalances, resulting in pancreatitis, obesity, and gastrointestinal upset. Always place your cat's food out of reach of your puppy.

- Onions will kill off your dog's red blood cells, causing anemia. So if you are tempted to give your dog some baby food, read the label and make sure that there is no onion powder in the ingredients.

- There is some debate over the addition of garlic to your dog's food. In most forms, garlic can be just as deadly as onions; however, there are a few pet companies out there that are offering air-dried garlic granules for dogs. These supplements are said to offer protection against fleas, ticks, and mosquitoes. When it comes to garlic, do your homework and talk to your vet before adding any supplementation to your dog's diet. In an article by Anna Burke (2018), studies found that it takes 15 to 30 grams of garlic per kilogram of body weight to cause any harmful changes. Considering that the average supermarket clove is between three and seven grams, your dog would have to eat a considerable amount before becoming sick. However, you should know that some dogs are more sensitive to garlic toxicity, and a few days of buildup could lead to a potential problem.

- Caffeine is a dangerous thing for your dog and can be found in energy drinks, coffee, tea, cocoa, chocolate, and colas. It can even have a presence in cold medicine and painkillers. So if your dog has somehow ingested caffeine, get them to the vet as soon as possible.

- Who knew that fruit could cause a problem, but grapes and raisins can cause kidney failure in dogs, even in small amounts. So if you are growing grapes in your backyard, you should remove those vines immediately.

- Whether raw or roasted, it only takes six macadamia nuts to make your pup sick. Keep watch for muscle shakes, vomiting, high temperatures, and weakness in the hind legs. Contact your vet right away.

- Skip the milk and dairy if you suspect your pup has a food allergy. It can cause diarrhea and digestive issues if they are sensitive.

. . .

- Mushrooms, depending upon the species, can be extremely toxic to dogs. So play it safe and skip mushrooms! They can bring serious illness and death.

- Most people know that any form of chocolate is bad for dogs. It causes heart problems, seizures, tremors, and death.

- Fruits with seeds or pits, like persimmons, can cause a blockage in your dog's intestines, and pits from plums or peaches should never be allowed to be chewed on. They contain cyanide and can block intestines. Not to mention they could crack a tooth!

- Raw eggs can be a bit of a debate. Some people swear by raw eggs, but, as far as the medical community is concerned. Raw egg whites can risk the development of salmonella or E. coli. Always ask your nutritionist if you have questions.

- Even though dogs and bones seem like a natural combination, many bones will splinter and cause cuts or block your dog's delicate digestive system. Also, fat trimmings, whether raw or uncooked, are never recommended because they can cause pancreatitis.

- Every living creature indeed needs some kind of salt in their diet, but giving your dog or puppy food like chips or pretzels can cause some severe issues because of the high salt content. Remember to keep those chip bags out of reach and cut them up before placing them in the garbage. Pet suffocation is heartbreaking and easily avoided.

. . .

- Watch the sugar intake. Too much of a good thing can cause diabetes and problems with their teeth.

- If you have a counter surfer, you will have to take extra care about what your dog can access from your countertops. Bread dough that contains yeast will need to rise and, if your dog eats it during this phase, it will swell and cause your dog a lot of pain. Yeast will also ferment, so it could trigger alcohol poisoning.

- Your dogs should never take any of your medications unless the vet says it is okay to do so. Medications that seem harmless to you could prove deadly to your dog.

If you suspect that your dog has ingested something toxic, contact the National Animal Poison Control Center.

How to Switch to a Different Food

At one point or another, we all want to try a different food for whatever reason. Any time that you change dog foods make sure that it is a gradual change. Dogs' digestive systems can be delicate, and they are used to the same diet every meal, unlike us humans that eat something different every night. Ideally, you will make this change over a week, blending one food with another until your dog has a chance to adjust to the change. The common standard when changing foods is:

- Day 1: 75% old food and 25% new food
- Day 3: 50% old food and 50% new food
- Day 5: 25% old food and 75% new food
- Day 7: 100% new food

. . .

If your dog has a more sensitive digestive system, you should keep in mind that you may want to extend this transition period, making the change in smaller increments and perhaps increasing the time to two weeks or a bit longer. If you follow the guidelines and your dog still seems to be exhibiting signs of digestive upset, you may need to consult a nutritionist or your vet as an allergy to an ingredient, and the third choice of food may be in order.

5

SOCIALIZING – RAISING A FRIENDLY PUPPY

Puppies have so much potential, curiosity, and intelligence. That's why puppy training begins when your puppy comes into your house — whether you want it to or not. Soiling, biting, jumping, barking, and running are natural behaviors; as a new puppy parent, it is up to you to demonstrate where and when those behaviors are appropriate and, more importantly, where they are inappropriate. Begin teaching and socializing your puppy as early as eight weeks of age if properly vaccinated and your veterinarian confirms his good health. Although the techniques in this chapter are best suited for puppies two to four months of age, you'll find the information valuable when training older puppies, too.

Why Socializing Is So Important

This chapter will detail why socialization is important for so many parts of your dog's life, but here's an example to help you understand. You bring home your pup on a long weekend so that you and your family can spend the first few days with him and get your schedule off to a successful start. You have a dog walker lined up so that when it's time to go back to work and school, your pup will continue to be well taken care of. When your real-life work, school, and other activities settle into a routine, you continue to walk your growing pup in the morning and evening, and your kids play with him in the afternoon, often with friends. He learns Sit, Down, Stay, Wait, and Off, and besides some accidents in the house, things seem to be going well. Your pup/dog is always happy to see you, sleeps in your room, plays nicely with the kids, and seems well adjusted.

THEN YOU DECIDE he can come along on a holiday weekend to your in-laws' house. They also have a dog, and you are excited to introduce your dog to theirs. You finally arrive at their house, and everyone piles out of the car to excitedly say hello. You put your pup on a leash to introduce him, and your in-laws' dog comes bounding out of the house to greet everyone. He is a pleasant but large dog. When your puppy sees him, he wants to bolt. He doesn't know what to do. His fear causes the other dog to assume an aggressive stance, and your pup responds in either fear or aggression. There is a squabble, and everyone is upset. As the weekend goes on, your dog has accidents in the house, especially when several people are in the same room together. When strange kids want to pet him, he runs away or, worse, snaps at them. You are upset and reprimand, then punish your pup, exacerbating rather than appeasing him. You return home wondering if getting a dog was such a good idea and whether your dog will ever be able to go on trips with you.

Meeting People

Socialize your puppy to people, making sure he gets plenty of experiences with both genders and a variety of races and ages. For example, go to the park, a parade, the beach, outside of a shopping center, or an airport. Bring some of your puppy's kibble or some other tasty treats, and have strangers ask your puppy to sit for a greeting and a treat. If you do this often enough, your puppy will start to think, “If I sit when I see someone coming, I'll get a treat.” Not a bad thought!

. . .

ALLOWING friendly puppies to interact with friendly children — even toddlers — is great for both when the experience is positive. To ensure success, keep a careful eye on the pup and the child. It can be pure magic.

OCCASIONALLY, leave your puppy in the care of a trustworthy, level-headed friend for a minute, an hour, or a day. Your objective is to teach the pup to be self-assured in your absence; therefore, don't say goodbye or hello to the puppy. Treat the situation as a nonevent, so your puppy is less likely to experience separation anxiety.

THINK about items people carry and the equipment they use. Expose your puppy to wheelchairs, canes, bicycles, lawnmowers, roller skates, vacuum cleaners, etc.

Getting to Know the World

Help your puppy become a savvy traveler accustomed to elevators, stairways, manholes, and grates. Acclimate him to walking on various surfaces such as gravel, wire, sand, cobblestone, linoleum, and brick. Because some puppies prefer to eliminate only in their backyard, teach him to eliminate on command in different areas, so weekend trips and the like won't be a problem.

IF YOU WANT to foster enjoyment of the water and your puppy isn't a natural pond-puppy, walk him on a leash along the shoreline. Once he is at ease with that, venture into the water. Gently tighten the leash as you go, forcing him to swim a couple of feet before you let him return to the shoreline. Never throw any puppy into the water.

. . .

Why is confidence so important when it comes to training and raising your puppy?

A confident dog allows guests in the house with little fanfare but will always be alert should something go wrong. The confident dog does not shy away from people or act skittish. He is sure of himself and can be depended upon for a steady temperament. He is not overly aggressive toward strangers or other dogs. A skittish dog, a dog that lacks confidence, is unsure of people or other dogs. His behavior can be unpredictable.

Meeting Other Animals

Let him get to know other animals — cats, chickens, horses, goats, birds, guinea pigs, lizards, and of course, other puppies and dogs. Upon meeting a new species, a puppy is often startled, then curious, and finally, some become bold or aggressive. For his protection and the protection of the other animal, always keep him leashed so you can control his distance and stop unwanted behaviors by enforcing obedience commands.

Whatever you are socializing your puppy to — animals, objects, or people — approach the new thing in a relaxed manner and avoid any situation that would intimidate the average puppy, such as a group of grade-schoolers rushing at him. Be prepared for three reactions: walking up to check it out and sniff, apprehensive barking with hackles raised, or running away.

No matter how well-socialized your pup may be, there will be situations where it would be unfair to trust him to ignore his instincts. For example, if your niece has a pet mouse and you have a Dachshund or a terrier, you can't expect that the mouse could safely play outside of its cage with your dog in the room. These dogs have been bred through time to hunt down such small animals.

No matter his response, remain silent. In the first (and, by the way, best) scenario, he is thinking rationally and investigating his environment — don't draw attention to yourself by talking, praising, or petting. Allow him to explore uninterrupted. This good boy is entertaining himself and being educated at the same time. If your puppy lacks confidence or displays fear, don't console him because this will reinforce his fear. Instead, use the leash to prevent him from running away. If he is still slightly uncomfortable, drop some tasty bits of food (like slivers of hot dog) on the ground. Most puppies will relax after a nibble or two because the uncomfortable situation has been positively associated with food.

If loud noises frighten your puppy, desensitize him by allowing him to create a racket. Offer him a big metal spoon with a little peanut butter on it. Give him an empty half-gallon or gallon milk jug with the cap removed and a bit of squeeze cheese in the rim to bat around. It won't be long before he is creating unrest and loving it. Of course, if the clamoring drives you nuts, feel free to limit his playtime with these items. Also, socialize your puppy to walk on a leash, ride in the car, and be examined and groomed.

When introducing a new puppy to your current dog or cat, remember that your established pet considers your home its territory. If possible, try to introduce the animals in neutral territory, maybe in a friend's yard. It's very important to make sure neither of the animals becomes afraid of the other, or the other pet will quickly become a bully.

Riding in the Car

As soon as your puppy is large enough, teach him to enter and exit the car on command. Practice this by leashing him, walking him up to the car, and commanding him to go in as you give him a boost. Next, invite him out of the car by calling Come as you gently pull the leash. Practice several of these several times a day until he goes in and out on command. Even before your puppy is ready for that lesson, decide where you'd like him to ride. Crating is the safest option. If it isn't the most convenient, try a puppy seatbelt available at many pet shops or by mail order. Don't feed your puppy for hours before riding if he has any tendency toward carsickness. It is also prudent to keep the air temperature inside the car comfortably cool (if you roll down a window, choose one that your puppy cannot stick his head out of). Additionally, you'll reduce the chance of motion sickness by avoiding bumpy roads and abrupt stops or turns.

LEAVING a dog in an unattended car in the summer is extremely dangerous. Remember that just because it's cloudy now doesn't mean the sun won't poke through any minute. Whenever you take your dog with you to run errands, be sure to have a place to tie your dog up outside; even cracking all the windows won't help much as the temperature in your car can climb well above 100 degrees quickly.

Rules for Young Children with New Puppies

It is best practice never to leave your puppy and a young child together unsupervised, regardless of the breed of the dog. Both the child and the dog can be unpredictable.

WHEN YOU INTRODUCE a puppy into your family, children must know how to handle the puppy.

. . .

They must learn that it is **not** OK to pull the puppy's ears or tail. To prevent anxiety and food aggression, children also need to know that the puppy should not be disturbed while eating his food.

Remember that when you introduce a new family member into the fold, this can be threatening to your dog and needs to be done with a lot of thought and sensitivity, ensuring it is done carefully and safely.

6

TRAINING ON MANNERS - OBEDIENCE TRAINING

The Name Game

The purpose is to teach your puppy their name and to focus on you.

THIS GAME REINFORCES the idea that you are awesome. You are always at the top and always worth paying attention to, regardless of what else is happening around your puppy.

FOR THIS TRAINING, you are going to need mild distractions. If your puppy isn't paying attention to you at all, your environment is too distracting; find somewhere else.

PLACE YOUR PUPPY ON A LEASH, an arm's length away—not the full length of the leash. It doesn't matter if they are standing, sitting, or lying down. You should be able to touch the tip of their nose while you remain standing or seated if you're unable to stand.

If you have a helper, the other person should create a mild distraction such as walking through the room or making noise from another room such as crinkling a bag or coughing, or bouncing a ball (any noise other than calling the dog's name).

If you are solo, set up your training area with naturally occurring distractions such as a yard with distant squirrels or passing delivery trucks.

As soon as your puppy turns their attention to the distraction, immediately call their name once—only once—in a happy voice.

If they whip their head to look in the general vicinity of your face, say *Yes* (verbal marker) and give them a treat.

If they don't look at you when you say their name, put a treat in front of their nose so they can smell it, then pull it up to your eyes. You should be standing straight up or sitting, not down at their level. Once they look up at you, say *Yes* and give the treat.

Do two to five minutes of repetitions of this game during each session, which you can repeat several times throughout the day. This game should be upbeat and fast-paced.

. . .

Only use *one* name for your puppy, not a bunch of different pet names. For a puppy, it's too confusing to learn different commands and names. When they're older, your dog will learn via context and repetition that "Snowflake" and "Snowy" and "Snowball" and "Snow Snow" are all meant for them, but for now, just pick one.

Obedience Training

Obedience training is the art of training your puppy to obey your commands. Dogs are pack animals, and they look to their pack leader to tell them what to do. The key to successful dog training is to set yourself up as the pack leader. The best way to help your dog learn is to start when he is young and use consistent practice. For example, try training just before a meal; that way, your pup will come to his meal as a reward. It will also make him more likely to comply with your commands. Remember that puppies are young and active, so keep your training sessions short and make sure they are not hungry or tired.

Following are basic obedience commands that every dog should know.

Obedience Training: Teaching to Heel

Teaching your puppy how to heel is important, especially when there are other dogs around or people that your dog might want to jump on without invitation. When you command your dog to heel, the dog will sit by your side quietly until released. This is difficult for puppies to learn, especially since they are so energetic and curious by nature.

The key to this part of puppy training is, of course, treats. Start by standing with your puppy on a leash and keep a few treats in the hand that isn't holding the leash. The puppy needs to understand the command, so tell your dog to heel. Once he sits still next to you for about five seconds, give the dog a treat. Then, take five steps forward and allow your dog to follow. Say the word "heel" and wait for your puppy to sit down next to you. Reward with a treat. Continue doing this, so your puppy understands. The dog will associate your movements and words with the expected behaviors.

ONCE THIS IS COMPLETED in the exact location, introduce some other people and distractions. You might feel like you're starting the process all over again, but that's only because your puppy will notice those other people or bouncing balls or moving cars. Repeat the process with the treats until your dog is obedient and able to heel on command.

Obedience Training: Teaching to Sit

Teaching your puppy to sit is not complicated, and the dog will understand what you want when you reward with treats and physically show the animal what you expect. When you teach a puppy to sit, you are not only teaching him that you are in charge, but that if he wants any type of reward, he is going to have to sit on the ground and behave.

THIS ALSO KEEPS dogs from jumping up on people. It's also a great way to ensure the puppy does not take food from people's hands in the house.

THE FIRST THING is to get a treat for your puppy. Make sure you have a quiet place to train your dog that is free from any distractions. Stand in front of your puppy and hold your hand above his head with a treat in it. He will look up at it. Use your other hand to gently push down on his hindquarters until he's in a sitting position. At the same time, while still holding the treat, say "sit" in a calm but firm voice. Once he can hold the position, give the puppy the treat.

REPEAT this process about ten more times. If the puppy is sitting for you when the treat is held above his head, you are ready to move on to the next step. If not, continue repeating this step until the dog sits on command.

THE NEXT STEP is to hold your hand out without the treat and tell your puppy to sit. If the dog sits, reward him with three treats, then take a break.

THE NEXT DAY, start with the empty-handed motion while repeating the word "sit" and providing the puppy with one treat. When you are sure the puppy fully grasps the sit command, you can choose to stop saying sit and use only the hand motion to get the dog to sit, providing treats each time he obeys.

MAKE sure your puppy understands the command completely. However, as we all know, we cannot continue to feed the dog treats every time we tell him to do something. Therefore, you need to begin cutting back on the number of treats you give the puppy. One way to do this is to give your puppy a treat every other time he obeys the command, then every third time, and so on, until you are no longer giving the dog a treat for sitting.

BE sure only to teach your puppy one command at a time. Once the dog understands that command, continue to practice for five minutes each day. As you practice, increase the distractions the puppy is exposed to while you tell him to sit, which will prepare him for the distractions he will face outside of your home, or when he becomes excited and needs to be brought under control.

You can also practice telling your puppy to sit in the middle of playtime. Run around with your puppy, playing, and then stop suddenly and tell him to sit.

If your puppy temporarily loses the training you've mastered, simply start again.

Obedience Training: Teaching to Lie Down

The next command is the lie-down command. It is a good command for your puppy to learn so you can keep him in one spot and help calm him. This is also an excellent way to handle barking.

Once again, find a quiet place to teach your puppy the command. Begin by telling your puppy to sit, show the dog the treat in your hand, bring it down to the floor, and say “down.” It is a good idea to close the treat in your fist when you bring it down to the floor, so the puppy will know that it is there but that he's not allowed to take it from you. As the puppy lowers his body down to the floor in the lying position, give him the treat.

Bring your puppy back to the sitting position and repeat the process about ten times. After the dog has gotten used to getting a treat for lying down, you can stop bringing your hand to the floor, but instead, simply tell the puppy to lie down. If the dog does as he is told, give him three treats. If not, go back to the first step until he understands that the command “lie down” is followed by the treat, and try again.

. . .

After he has followed the command without you having to lower your hand to the floor, take a break. The next day, practice ten times, having the dog lie down without bringing your hand to the floor.

Again, after the puppy has mastered this, begin reducing the number of treats the dog receives until the dog no longer receives treats for the behavior.

Obedience Training: Teaching to Stay

Teaching a puppy to stay is problematic because it's counterintuitive to a puppy who wants to explore and jump and sniff and bark. The stay command is vital for your puppy to learn because it will teach him self-control and help ensure the dog does not bolt out the front door when you are trying to leave.

Teach your dog the stay command after he has mastered the sit and lie-down commands. Find a quiet place for you to train the dog. Begin by commanding your puppy to sit. After the dog is in the sit position, tell the dog to "stay," wait two seconds, and then give the dog a treat. Increase the amount of time you make the dog wait for the treat until the dog can wait for ten seconds, each time, telling the dog to stay.

Each time you say "stay," put up your hand, flat, with the palm facing the dog. This will become your hand command once your dog learns how to stay. If the dog gets up from the sitting position, say "no," have the dog sit again, and start the process over.

. . .

When the dog can stay in the sitting position for ten seconds without getting up, continue the process, but this time take one step away from the dog. Repeat the word “stay.” Take two more steps, and again repeat the word “stay.” Finally, step out of the dog’s sight.

Continue to work with the puppy until you can stay out of the dog’s sight for two minutes without him moving. After the puppy has mastered this skill, start again, but this time begin with the lie-down position and have the dog learn to stay from there.

Obedience Training: Teaching to wait

Before proceeding, we should explain how ***Wait*** is different from ***Stay***. ***Wait*** is incredibly versatile, for the myriad times you’d like them to be polite and patient, such as waiting calmly to get their dinner, or pausing at the door instead of bolting out, or not jumping out of the car and potentially into ongoing traffic. In a ***Wait***, your puppy remains calmly in position until you release them with a release word.

Stay is used in formal obedience and rarely used in day-to-day life. A dog in a ***Stay*** must remain in that position until you come back to them. It means, “I’m leaving, don’t move, I’ll be back.”

To teach *Wait*, you will need a new kind of marker, a verbal release word. Many people use “Okay,” but we advise against it because puppies hear you use this word all the time, so it lacks specialness. We like the words "free" and "release." We’ll use the word ***Free*** as the verbal release word in this book. Whatever you choose, remember always to be consistent.

. . .

To teach ***Wait***, the optimal time is dinnertime. Your puppy should be good and hungry.

Take your dog's food bowl off the floor and fill it with their dinner. Walk over to where they usually eat.

While holding the bowl in one hand, with your other hand, put your puppy into a ***Sit*** or a ***Down*** (***Sit*** is most common). As a reminder, you'll hold a treat in your hand and guide it back over your puppy's head to lead them into the sit. They should be arm's length from the bowl.

Give the hand gesture of a flat palm toward the puppy's face like a stop signal and say ***Wait*** once and only once.

With your puppy now sitting politely, put the bowl down.

If they break the sit, use your nonresponse marker (***Ah ah***) and pull the food bowl back up off the floor. Reset by putting them back into a sit (Step 2). Repeat Steps 2 to 5 as many times as needed, keeping very matter-of-fact and without showing any hint of frustration. Whatever you do, don't allow them to eat their food until you have put the bowl down and stood up straight with them remaining in the sit position.

If they stay sitting while you stand back up, give the release word ***Free***, and they should now enjoy their dinner. You don't need to say ***Yes*** or give a treat; dinner is their reward.

. . .

If your puppy doesn't release when you say ***Free***, tap on the food bowl and say, "It's okay, you can eat!" Keep it happy, cheerful, and encouraging. In a moment, they'll come over and dine.

Most commonly, the moment you put that bowl on the floor, your puppy is going to break their sit and try to bury their face in the bowl. Do your utmost not to let that happen; be nimble and ready to snatch that bowl back up off the floor. But if they do rush past your defenses and manage to snag a few pieces of kibble, that's okay. Don't despair, but pull the bowl up anyway, as that ***Wait*** just wasn't good enough.

Obedience Training: Teaching to Come

Puppies always want to come when they're called. They want to know what you're up to, and they're going to be eager to be close to you and be a part of whatever you're doing. However, it can be difficult to get your puppy to come if it is preoccupied with something else. Maybe the puppy is digging in the backyard or stalking a squirrel or utterly obsessed with the scent on some random car's tires. The trick is to teach the dog that coming to you is the best decision that could ever be made. When you call your puppy's name, and your little buddy comes running over, shower that dog with praise and love and treats. With that kind of affection and positive reinforcement, your puppy will never want to miss the opportunity to come to you when called.

For training purposes, call your puppy from one room to another. When your puppy is in the living room, stand in the kitchen and call the dog by name. When your puppy comes running, get excited, pet him, and provide a treat. When the puppy can understand that coming when called means only positive things, he will obey immediately.

Obedience Training: Teaching "No"

You teach your puppy the "no" command only when he exhibits bad behavior. Training your puppy to respond to the "no" word can save you a lot of trouble. The steps used to teach a dog the "no" command are similar to the other basic commands. First of all, whenever you find your puppy doing something unwanted, such as jumping on the sofa or barking, immediately clap your hands and say, “No,” at the same time. Clapping your hands will distract your dog from what he is doing and most likely stop his action. Be sure to say the word "no" in a firm, loud voice, but only say it once because you're training the dog to listen the first time. If the puppy obeys, give him a treat and a lot of praise, and redirect the dog to something else. For example, if he is chewing on a piece of clothing, give him a toy. Again, consistency and patience are required. You won't be able to train your new puppy overnight. However, with time and structure, obedience training can be conquered.

Obedience Training: Teaching "Leave It"

Teaching your dog the command “leave it” is essential. It could save his life if he were to pick up something potentially toxic to him, dangerous, or something important to you – that you don’t want him to destroy. Make sure that you try your best to set him up for success. Tailor the lessons that you do together so that he will earn a reward instead of failing. This will help you both by keeping both of you from being frustrated.

HIDE some small treats in both of your hands (close fists). Have your dog sit in front of you. When he sniffs one of your hands, say, “leave it.” You must choose one phrase and stick to it. Don’t swap back and forth; you have to stay consistent.

. . .

Praise him and reward him from your fist (the one he wasn't sniffing) when he stops and looks away from your fist. Repeat this when he no longer tries to sniff your hands. This is the first part that you and your dog have to master before moving on.

The next step is to hide small treats in your closed fists and say the command. Then open one of your hands to show him the treat but close it if he gets close and tries to take the treat. Repeat these steps until he tries his best to ignore the treat from your open hand. Once this happens, give him praise and reward him. Repeat this second part until this response happens instantly.

Next – while you and your dog sit on the floor – set the treat on the floor near you and say "leave it" (or whatever command you choose). If he tries to get it from the floor, cover it with your hand. When he looks away, give him praise and reward him (with a different treat). Repeat this process until you are confident that he does the desired behavior instantly.

The next part is to have your dog sit in front of you while you are standing. Leave the treat on the floor close to you and say "Leave it" (or whatever command you chose). If he tries to take the treat, cover it with your foot. When he looks away from it or tries to ignore the treat, give him praise and reward him with a different treat. Repeat this part until you believe that he can respond to the desired behavior instantly.

This next part is to walk past the treat while he is on a leash. Make sure you say the command "leave it" or whichever words you choose. Use the leash to keep him from getting the treat if you need to. Once he ignores the treat on the floor, give him some praise and a different treat. Repeat until you think he's instantly doing this desired behavior.

TWO MORE STEPS, and we'll be done! This next one is to say "leave it" while not on a leash. This may or may not be difficult, depending on how your dog does with all of the previous practice. The more you practice, the easier this part will be. Be prepared to step in front of him or snatch the treat away if he tries to grab it.

THE LAST PART is to practice this with different items on the floor. Remember that you will need to practice this command each week, even if you think he has mastered it. Even just a short session each week will help him learn.

Leash Training

Puppies thrive on excitement and are curious creatures. It would be best to remember that walking on a leash is not an instinctive behavior for a dog or puppy, so it must be learned. If you have dreams of your puppy staying right by your side, don't be upset when they pull away to chase an errant leaf, cricket, or piece of paper that crosses their path. The first venture out of your yard will bring new smells and experiences into your puppy's world, and they may become overstimulated with everything going on around them. Don't be discouraged if they have trouble remembering their basic commands on their first few ventures out. Also, straining on the end of the leash and pulling is exciting, but you have just rewarded their behavior if you give in and run with them. Let's snap that leash on your puppy and get ready to walk!

WHEN INTRODUCING the leash to your new puppy, they may think that it's a toy to be chewed upon, but it won't take long before realizing that the leash means 'go for a walk.' The jangling of the leash will become one of the essential sounds to fill your dog's world and can wake them from a solid slumber in less than a second. Hopefully, they will hold still while you try and attach the leash, but puppies can be wiggly at times. Stay patient; this experience is like Christmas every day for a toddler.

HOPEFULLY, you have successfully taught your dog the sit command so that they will hold still for their leash to be attached to their collar or harness. If they are overstimulated, wait until they have calmed down and try to connect the leash again. Your puppy must learn to hold still because trying to leash a moving target will become a trying task.

ONCE YOU ARE both ready to begin your first journeys, it is best to choose a short route in your neighborhood and practice walking it regularly. Keeping your puppy in a pleasant and familiar walk routine will provide less stimulation than new routes and smells. This practice will aid you in the teaching of proper habits while walking on their leash. If you are lucky enough to already have a trained dog within your household, they will be able to help your puppy understand what is expected of them.

IF YOU FIND that your puppy is still overstimulated on your routine walk and is pulling harder than you would like, you could try having a training session or playing a game of fetch beforehand. A dog that has participated in some form of exercise before its walk may be less inclined to pull you around the block. Your new mantra will be, "**a good puppy is a tired puppy.**"

. . .

Depending upon your breed of puppy, they can be powerful, leading to unwanted pulling. To control their speed, one trick you can try is increasing your walking pace. Your puppy will want to stay with you and be less inclined to go off to follow a fascinating smell.

Any time that your puppy displays a good behavior remember to reward them. When working on desired leash skills, here are a few methods that may help you.

Follow the Treat

Thank heavens that most dogs are food-oriented; bribery makes it so much easier for owners to get desired behaviors. Always keep your treat pouch full and at least one in your hands. When you begin your walk, hold your hand with the treats right in front of their hyper-sensitive nose. Their sense of smell will tell them precisely what you are holding, and now you have their interest. When you walk your puppy, you want them to focus on you and turn to look at you as if they need to gain your approval every so often. When you call their name, and they perform the act of making eye contact, pop a treat in their mouth and tell them they are good.

If your puppy begins to pull or veer off, stop the walk and make your dog come to you and sit. When they perform this, give them plenty of praise and resume the walk, still holding the treats in front of their nose.

Somewhere around the two-week mark, you should experience some success using this method, and you can stop carrying treats in your hand and leave them in the training pouch. Over time, your pup will be able to walk further without pulling. You can still offer them treats for a job well done, but make it less frequent until you can phase the practice out entirely. Feel free to give your dog a treat on a walk every once in a while just to reinforce that they are pleasing you.

Stop-n-Go

Do you recall way back in grade school when you played red light, green light, dynamite, boom? This is the canine version of that game. Picture you are out walking your dog (green light) when they begin to walk away from you because their attention is focused on something that isn't you. You stop walking and do not allow them to go further (red light). Once the dog realizes that neither of you are going anywhere, they should stop walking. Command your dog to come (dynamite) and then sit (boom). Never give in until they give you the desired response, but positively do this. There is no shame in dipping into the treat pouch!

During the walk, should your puppy choose to stay by your side, praise and reward them. With repetition and hard work, they will eventually stop pulling, and your walks should become enjoyable for both of you. Your pup should learn that walking pleasantly earns them yummy rewards.

Throw in a Surprise Turn

While this is not a preferred technique, this method can be used as long as your dog is not wearing a slip lead device or a head halter. Following this particular train of thought can put undesirable pressure on their neck if done improperly.

The idea behind this technique is to toss in a surprise when your dog tests the end of the leash and pulls. Always try to give them a verbal warning first to see if that is enough to slow them down or return to your side. Should that work, that's great, and praise them, but if they don't, then it's time for you to turn around and begin walking in the opposite direction. If done properly, your arm will take the brunt of the movement, and your dog should only feel a light tug on their harness or collar.

Continue in the opposite direction until your dog catches up to you, then praise them. Now you can both turn back to the original direction. You can repeat these steps as often as needed, provided you ask gently. If the previous two leash training techniques are not working, this is the next alternative. If your dog becomes upset and shows you signs of being frightened, stop this method and try a different approach.

The Half Halt Method

If done incorrectly, this technique could be considered negative reinforcement. It must be done gently and without yanking or constant pressure.

Lace the leash alternately in between your fingers and, should your puppy pull or try to get too far ahead of you, gently squeeze the leash, causing a gentle tug on the collar or harness. This can be used multiple times in a row, but not with any force. It is meant as a reminder and not as any sort of punishment, and you can add vocal reminders along with the action.

Any sort of hard tugging can result in physical damage to your dog's neck or throat. There are many 'no pull' harnesses on the market that clip in the front of your dog's chest. Some have proven successful, and if you are having difficulties, you may want to spend some time researching different brands. Always choose humane methods while using patience and repetition.

TOGETHER, you both will have miles of fun and adventure.

NOTE: I do not recommend retractable leashes. You have less control, and this encourages your dog to pull way out in front of you. This type of leash is dangerous and has been responsible for injuries to both dogs and owners.

7

CORRECTING BEHAVIOR PROBLEMS

If you're a puppy, you feel like the entire world has been created for you to enjoy. You want to play and run and bark and jump and bite. To become well-behaved household pets, puppies need to be trained in acceptable behavior and what it isn't. While it might be fun to watch your puppy acting cute, it's not fun to listen to barking, pick up scraps of what was once your favorite pair of slippers, or repair the once-landscaped backyard that has been dug to pieces. Behavior training for your puppy is necessary for your peace of mind and your little dog's protection.

Chewing

Chewing is a behavior that comes naturally to dogs; however, it can also cause damage. Puppies usually begin chewing because they explore the world with their mouths. However, they need to understand what is acceptable to chew on and what is off-limits because if they chew on the wrong thing, they can cost their owners a lot of money and may even cost them their lives.

. . .

It is also essential to understand that a puppy will chew more when he is teething, as this is an excruciating process, and chewing gives him some relief from the pain. If a puppy chews on the wrong items, it will most likely happen while he is teething. If chewing is not controlled during this time, it can become a tough habit to break later.

When teaching your puppy not to chew on inappropriate items, the first thing you should do when teaching your puppy not to chew on inappropriate items is to ensure no underlying medical conditions are causing the puppy to chew. There are specific dietary issues, parasites, and intestinal problems that can be the cause of this.

The next step is to puppy-proof your house. Look around your home to ensure your puppy does not have access to anything that might put his life in danger. Ensure all of the household chemicals are put up and away from the puppy and that all of the power cords are covered so the puppy cannot get to them. Remove any objects the puppy might find interesting, such as socks or shoes.

It is best to restrict the puppy to a small area in the home, such as the living room. You can do this by utilizing baby gates on the doorways inside of the living room. It will also make it easier for you to keep the puppy from getting into things he shouldn't.

Give your puppy items that are okay for him to chew on. Each dog will have a different preference for what they like, so it is good to provide him with a few extra toys of various textures. Be careful with rawhide and beef bones because the puppy can chew on these until a small piece breaks off that could fit inside his mouth and cause him to choke.

. . .

Make sure the toys you provide for your puppy are of the appropriate size. The dog must be able to pick the toy up quickly and carry it around. However, it needs to be big enough that he will not swallow it. If you purchase a toy with any type of hole in it, make sure the hole is not big enough for the dog to get his jaw stuck in it.

Do not give your puppy toys that look like items you don't want him to chew on. For example, many owners purchase a toy that looks like a shoe while telling the dog not to chew on shoes. You should also avoid giving the dog an old shoe to chew on if you hope to teach him not to chew on new shoes.

By providing the puppy with items that he can chew and keeping inappropriate items out of his reach, you will make a lot of progress to ensure that he does not wrap his teeth around anything inappropriate.

If you find the dog chewing on an item he should not be chewing on, you must take the thing away from him and state in a loud voice, "NO." Please put the item away so that he understands he is not supposed to chew on it. After taking the object away from the puppy, redirect his attention by providing him with one of the toys he can chew on.

Always make sure you praise the puppy for chewing on appropriate items to ensure he learns what he should and should not chew on. If you find the puppy has difficulty understanding which things he should not chew on, spray the item with Bitter Apple as a deterrent. If an item tastes bitter, the dog is less likely to chew on it.

. . .

You should also make sure your puppy is getting enough exercise. A bored dog is likely to search for items on which he can chew. Be sure to spend time each day taking your puppy for walks, playing with him, and just spending time together. Not only will this make the bond between the two of you stronger, but it will also ensure the puppy does not destroy items that are important to you.

Barking

The next behavior to get under control is barking—Dogs bark for a variety of reasons. Most owners eventually learn what each of their dog's barks means. For example, a dog may bark in a specific way if he needs to go outside, he will bark differently if he needs food or water, and he will bark in another way if he wants to play.

Dogs also bark to warn other animals to stay away, to sound an alarm warning their owner of danger, or just because they want to bark.

Of course, you don't want to stop your puppy from every kind of barking. It is best to make sure the dog can warn you of danger or scare off anyone or anything that could harm you, but stop it from barking over you when you are talking or sleeping at night.

Your aim should be to stop the puppy from barking when there is no reason for him to bark. Many people make the huge mistake of paying attention to the dog when it barks or tell it to be quiet in a loud voice, which makes the dog think you are proud of his barking, and to him, you are joining in with the barking as you "bark" loud commands for him to be quiet.

. . .

To get your puppy's barking under control, you must first get to know the dog so you can begin to understand what situations might cause him to bark. When you know why he barks, you will be able to control the situation and show the dog you are a confident leader for him to follow.

From the moment you get the dog, you have to build a strong bond with him. He has to be able to trust you and know you will take control of any situation.

There are several ways for you to control unnecessary barking. Some people recommend holding the dog's mouth gently closed when he is barking. It is not the best way to teach your dog not to bark. Other people think you should keep the dog's mouth busy with a toy; however, you must be careful if you use this approach because the dog may think he is being rewarded for the barking behavior.

It would be best if you taught your puppy the “quiet” command. Consistently say “quiet” in a firm and calm voice when you want him to stop barking. After he stops barking, reward him with praise and a treat. After he has mastered the command, begin giving treats less often until you no longer provide treats for this behavior.

Some barking can be ignored. Expect some barking when you first crate train a puppy, as he's getting used to his surroundings and will try to do whatever he can to get you to take him out of the crate. The barking will cease with time and can be ignored for the most part.

. . .

The barking you should not ignore is when the dog barks for the sake of barking. Barking in and of itself can be rewarding for the dog, as he is having fun, and if you allow him to continue, he will think it is okay.

When you take your puppy outside, be sure not to allow him to bark at those passing by or run the fence line, chasing cars as they pass by. When you show the dog you are the one in control of his behavior, he will accept that you decide when and where he can bark.

Biting

There are many reasons why dogs become aggressive and bite. The dog may feel overexcited or threatened. A lot of dog aggression comes from a lack of confidence and positive training. It would be best to socialize your dog with different people, dogs, children, and environments. Socialization will boost his confidence and reduce his fear in new settings.

Teaching a puppy not to bite is vital. Most people do not enjoy playing with a dog known for mouthing, chewing, or biting on hands, clothing, or other body parts. You need to get this type of behavior under control early on; as the puppy gets older, it is much less likely he will be sensitive to your reaction when he bites. Typically, an adult dog biting or chewing on people was not taught to be gentle when he was a puppy.

Mouthing is a natural behavior for dogs since they explore the world with their mouths. Biting, on the other hand, is a reaction to either fear or frustration.

. . .

MAKE sure you can tell the difference between playful mouthing and aggressive biting. You see, most people enjoy wrestling with their dogs, and they have no problem placing their hands in the dogs' mouths, which helps to build trust between the people and their dogs. Owners need to know that their dogs are not going to bite them viciously. When a dog is play-mouthing, the dog's body will be relaxed, his tail will wag, and although his face may be wrinkled, it is evident from his behavior that he is not aggressive.

AN ANGRY OR FRIGHTENED DOG, on the other hand, will have a stiff body, his muscles will be tense, and his tail will be straight. Most of the time, the dog will mouth a person before the bite as a warning, but this is not always the case.

IF YOU WANT to teach your puppy not to bite or mouth your body parts or clothing, spend some time playing with him. Allow the puppy to mouth your hand as you play, but as soon as he does, let out a yelp as if the puppy has seriously hurt you, and allow your hand to go limp, startling your dog.

THIS SHOULD IMMEDIATELY STOP the puppy from mouthing your hand. Praise the dog for stopping. You will often find that the dog will lick your hand. Resume play, and repeat the process if the dog mouths you again. Play with your pup for about fifteen minutes. Continue to do this every day until the dog no longer mouths you.

MOUTHING IS another reason why it is important to provide your puppy with a wide variety of chew toys of different textures. When the puppy has the toys, he is much less likely to bite during playtime.

Digging

Some dogs will turn their owner's yards upside down, making the owner feel as if they are doing it all on purpose. However, dogs dig for various reasons, none of them being to get revenge on their owners. Dogs dig because they are bored, looking for attention, hunting prey, entertaining themselves, or seeking protection, to name a few reasons.

The first thing to do if you want to stop your puppy from digging is to find out why the dog is digging in the first place. If the dog is left alone and outside for long periods with no one to keep him company, he may begin digging. In this case, ensure that you go out and play with him. It is also a good idea to ensure that he has plenty of toys to play with. Ensure you are walking the puppy at least twice each day to guarantee he is getting enough exercise and stimulation.

If your puppy is digging for prey, it will most likely be near the roots of trees. You can take steps to fence the animal out or use humane ways to catch the animal and move it to a safer place. However, you should never use poison of any type because the poison can also hurt or kill your puppy.

Dogs will dig large holes to lay in if they are left outside in hot weather or shield themselves from the cold, wind, or rain. This means the dog is searching for comfort, as well as protection. To prevent this, make sure your puppy has adequate shelter while he is outside. You can also bring the dog inside more often, so he is protected from extreme weather.

. . .

Ensure that the dog has a full bowl of water and that there is no way for the bowl to flip over. If the dog prefers to lay in a hole in the ground, make sure he has an area in the yard where he can dig.

A dog may also dig to get attention, which usually happens when the dog does not get enough time with, or attention from the owner. The only way to stop this type of behavior is to provide the dog with the love and attention he deserves.

Dogs also dig as a way to escape. It can occur if the dog is trying to get something outside of the pen or trying to get away from something. So the first thing you need to do is figure out if he is trying to get to something outside of the pen and remove the item from his view. The next thing you need to do is make sure the pen is inviting and appealing to your dog.

You also need to think about your home as well. If the environment is stressful to the puppy, he may try to dig under the fence to get away. If there is a lot of yelling, arguing, and stress in the home, the puppy will feel it, and he won't be comfortable there. Make sure you do your best to provide your puppy with a safe and loving environment so he will not want to run away.

You can bury chicken wire under the fencing of the dog's pen but see to it that any sharp edges are turned outwards and away from the puppy. You can also place large rocks that have been partially buried at the bottom of the fence.

However, it would be best if you did not punish the puppy after digging because this will only cause him to feel more anxiety and make him want to get away.

Behavior training for puppies might seem overwhelming, but if you follow these tips, you'll have a well-behaved dog in no time!

Nipping

When dogs play with each other, they tend to use their mouths to grab and play with each other. In many situations, things can start to get rough, and when this happens to a person, it's often viewed as a threat or an attack even though the dog is simply playful.

Even adult dogs resort to nipping because their biting behavior wasn’t corrected. These behaviors should be corrected as they can be interpreted as an attack or a form of aggression by some strangers.

It should be distinguished from another type of nipping, which is more serious. In some cases, dogs just want to be left alone, and they will nip so they can be left alone. You can quickly notice this type of nipping as your dog will bare its teeth with the gums becoming very visible, start growling and snapping its teeth in the air.

This type of behavior usually happens when children haven't been trained yet to interact with older dogs. Most children don't have any idea about respecting the space of their pets. Most of them just look at dogs as cute and cuddly animals that they can hug all of the time. Dogs usually give off warning signals such as snapping for barking. When the dog feels threatened, it can snap. It, however, doesn’t mean that you have an aggressive dog. It only means that you have an untrained one.

. . .

This nipping behavior also happens to be familiar with dogs interacting with each other. If it seems out of character that your dog is snapping, your dog could be in some physical pain. Bring him to your veterinarian to check if there are no physiological issues.

To handle this type of behavior, you need to see what mood your dog is actually in. Watch out for warning signs when your dog feels threatened. In this case, your dog simply wants you to back off. You need to take things slowly and build some comfort for your dog. If your child is too rough with a dog, make sure he backs off slowly to give the dog the space it needs.

Let your child sit farther and offer your dog some treats so your dog will be the one to approach the child instead of the other way around. You can also have an object that it wants to play tug of war with. This is an excellent way to calm your dog down.

If this doesn't work, you can move it to another place, such as bringing it outside the house.

If your dog wants to interact with you, you'll need some time to train him in the right way so that he can play with you. Do this by teaching your dog how to play the suitable game of tug of war. This helps your dog figure out when it's acceptable to bite when they're playing.

Stay consistent at redirecting your dog's urge to nip on an acceptable object instead of a person's flesh. Your dog will eventually be able to change its behavior drastically.

. . .

The key is to distinguish between nipping when the dog feels threatened and when the dog simply wants to play. We can also observe your dog's body language. If you hear some kind of growling and you see the dog bear its teeth and gums with its ears pointed back and its body getting tense, that's probably a good sign that your dog doesn't want to play. If your dog looks relaxed and has the bow pose, then it's a good sign that it wants to play.

Training your dog and your loved ones consistently will almost always give you good results.

Eating Poop

Some dogs enjoy eating the pieces of other dogs or their own. Some dogs do this out of instinct, as female dogs will clean the feces of their offspring. This happens to be quite common in dogs that are younger than a year and six months. I know it sounds disgusting, and that is why this behavior must be corrected.

As always, you need to talk to your veterinarian to rule out medical issues such as coprophagia. Remember that you can control this behavior by controlling your dogs' environment at all times. Once you catch your dog doing this, you need to stop it by getting its attention towards you and reward your dog when it complies.

This just happens to be another variation of a command of your dog letting go of food or clothes that you don't want your dog to chew on. Most dogs tend to outgrow this behavior, but it is so much better to end it soon as feces can contain bacteria that can be harmful to your dog and you. Make sure to pick up your dog's waste and offer your dog treats after it poops. Make sure that your dog has no access to your garbage either.

Whining

A puppy whines for a variety of reasons. Maybe he needs to go potty. Perhaps it needs water. Perhaps it's hungry. Maybe he's craving for a walk in the park. These are all reasonable reasons for the puppy to whine, but sometimes the habit goes too far. That is, it whines whenever it needs something from you. It would be best if you never condoned such behavior. If you give in to what the puppy wants every time it whines, then you are teaching it to whine if it needs something.

To stop whining, make sure first that the puppy has no reason to whine. Ensure that he is provided with the necessities like food, water, treats, toys, and shelter.

The best strategy is not to give the puppy any attention when it whines. Pay him attention only when he goes quiet. The puppy will soon learn that whining is useless and it doesn't help in getting the things he wants.

If the whining still continues, maybe it's time to set an appointment with a vet or a dog behaviorist. It's possible that the puppy is whining because of a health problem.

Begging

Many dog owners are not aware of it, but the begging habits of their dogs are their fault. We often unknowingly encourage begging. Too much begging can also lead to other problems like obesity and digestive issues.

. . .

To address the problem, start by telling the dog to stay in a place during your eating time. Confine the dog in another room if necessary. If somehow he gets out and makes it to the dinner table, never give it food, not even scraps. If you are going to provide the puppy with the leftovers, do it only after everyone has finished eating. And don't just hand over the scraps to the puppy. Bring the leftovers to the puppy's feeding bowl.

Jumping on People

This behavior is usually a manifestation of your pet's delight to see you or your visitor. It is also a way to seek your attention or receive something from you. If you do not correct this behavior now, the habit will continue into adulthood.

To correct it, intentionally turn around and walk away from the puppy. Don't say anything.

More often than not, your puppy will approach you after you walk away. When it does, command it to sit down before it jumps on you again. Praise your pet, pat it on its head and offer a treat reward.

Practice this strategy until your puppy learns that you only give treats and praises when it shows good behavior and sits.

These are the most common behavior problems in puppies. Once your puppy starts displaying any of these bad habits, you should address them immediately before getting worse or leading to more problems. The good news is that puppies can be quick learners. With the right approach and proper training, fixing these problems shouldn't be too difficult.

8

PUPPY BASIC CARE

Feeding Your Puppy

Puppies grow quickly. Within a few months, your puppy will develop its muscles, bone structure, teeth, and immune system, as well as a shiny coat. A healthy and balanced diet is critical to make sure that your pup grows up healthy.

When you pick the puppy up from a breeder or shelter, they will give you nutritional information and tell you what the puppy has been eating and how often. Try to follow these instructions, as any sudden changes will cause stomach upset. First, stick to the food the puppy was on when you got him for at least a couple of weeks. Then, when you change his diet, mix a little of the new food with the old and gradually replace it with the new—do it over seven to ten days.

Your puppy needs feeding four times a day to start with. This is to give the puppy fuel for energy and to aid in development and growth.

By the time he reaches six months of age, your puppy should be on just two meals a day, so make sure to cut others out gradually.

Choosing a Healthy Diet

The array of dog foods available is mind-boggling, but not all foods will be suitable for your puppy. For example, not all dogs can tolerate beef-based foods, as it upsets their stomachs. You will only know this if your breeder has told you or you found out the hard way. Some people feed their dogs on complete dry food; others mix tinned meat with it. Dry food has particular benefits in that a good one is a complete meal with all the necessary minerals, proteins, vitamins, and other nutrients that your puppy needs.

Biscuits also help keep your puppy's teeth clean, and they have a much longer shelf life than tinned food. However, when your pup is small, you may want to stick to meat or biscuits soaked in a little warm milk or water to soften them up. His teeth will not be strong enough to cope with crunching hard biscuits.

Make sure you buy food to suit the age of your puppy. Adult food is not suitable for a puppy and, as he grows older, you will need to switch from puppy food to a junior mix. Each life stage contains a different mix of minerals, vitamins, and nutrients, and your pup must be fed the right one.

No matter what you feed the puppy, always make sure fresh drinking water is available throughout the day. You don't need to limit the amount because dogs will only drink when they are thirsty. This is even more important during warm spells or if your puppy is fed on a dry diet.

. . .

Try not to feed your puppy table scraps. Not only can some human food be harmful, but your puppy can also get fat. An obese puppy will have severe health problems. One rule of thumb—if you give your puppy leftover vegetables or potatoes, make sure you reduce his regular meal to compensate. Weigh your puppy weekly; if he puts on too much weight, you feed him too much.

Most dogs will eat whatever you put in front of them. If your puppy goes off its food for more than twenty-four hours, see a vet. If there are no health concerns, you may need to evaluate his diet. Never give a puppy food with bones in it, chocolate, or onions. If you feed him liver, limit the amount since it can cause an excess of vitamin A, which can poison the puppy.

Compared with canned dog food, dry food is more convenient and has a longer shelf life but contains less protein and is not delicious. To entice a puppy to eat, you can mix dry food with a bit of meat.

Picky Eaters

If your puppy won't eat and there are no obvious health issues, there is a chance that he is picky. If you think pickiness is the problem, put the normal food in the bowl and leave it for fifteen minutes. Leave your puppy alone for the entire fifteen minutes.

If the food isn't eaten, pick the food up and wait until the next mealtime. Do the same again if necessary. Your puppy will soon realize that no other options are available, and he will have to eat what's on offer. If he still hasn't eaten after forty-eight hours, go back to the vet.

. . .

Do make sure that freshwater is available.

Transporting a Puppy

After your puppy has had all the vaccinations, you might want to take him to the park or family get-togethers. The best and safest way to transport your pup is in a crate. Line the crate with some of your puppy's bedding, as it will make him feel more comfortable in there.

Traveling with a Puppy

If you are planning a road trip, look for hotels or resorts that allow dogs. Always ensure that your puppy has had the right vaccinations BEFORE you travel and carry his passport with you at all times, as well as the microchip certificate.

Before you go on a long journey with your puppy, go on several smaller ones first. You need to see how he travels. Gradually increase the length of the journeys over a while. Most dogs travel just fine, but some do get stressed out or ill.

Feed your puppy well before you travel. Plan regular stops along your route and let your puppy out to stretch his legs, take a bathroom break, and have a fresh drink of water. Never leave your puppy alone in the car, especially in extreme temperatures.

Grooming a Puppy

Grooming is as much about bonding with your puppy and building up trust as it is about keeping him clean and healthy. Regular grooming removes dirt and dead hair from the puppy, keeping his skin healthy as well as his coat. There is now evidence that grooming can even reduce the owner's blood pressure and stress.

A PUPPY'S coat is very different from that of an adult dog. It's shorter, softer, and much fluffier. Even if your pup doesn't need grooming, you must get him used to it, so start early.

IT IS essential to do this daily or at least three times a week. Be gentle as well. Too much pulling and harsh brushing will hurt the puppy, and he won't come to you in the future.

HAVE your puppy sit on your lap, cuddle, and make a fuss of him first, then start to brush him gently. Give praise often, stroking and talking to him in a soft and gentle voice. Only brush for two minutes, and then give your puppy a treat.

REPEAT this a few times a day to start with, gradually increasing the amount of time brushing. If the puppy decides that the brush is a plaything and tries to bite it, ignore him and look away. Do not look at your puppy but do not let go of the brush. It won't take him long to realize that biting stops your attention.

AFTER ABOUT FIVE or six days, start to groom the belly, ears, tail, and other sensitive areas but be very gentle and keep the first few sessions short. Touch his feet, examine his nails and toes. Look in his ears and gently open his mouth to have a look inside.

ONCE YOUR PUPPY has gotten used to the routine, move to groom on a table with a non-slip covering on it or a place on the floor. Always end each session with a treat and a lot of snuggles and pets. This way, your pup gets used to grooming and will grow up accepting it.

Bathing a Puppy

It isn't recommended that you bathe your dog more than twice a year. However, if you have a naughty puppy, you might find yourself cleaning him more often. To start with, you can bathe him once a week to get him used to it. Here's how to wash a puppy safely:

USE proper dog shampoo or human baby shampoo. If you use dog shampoo, follow the instructions carefully. If you use baby shampoo, only use a small amount and avoid getting it in his eyes or mouth.

USE the sink for a tiny puppy or a large plastic tub. As your pup grows, you will need to use the shower, bath, or even outside with the hose in warmer weather.

ATTACH A SHOWER PIPE to the tap and test that the water is warm but not too hot. Wet your puppy's coat thoroughly. Try not to get water in his eyes but make sure you part the hair so that the water goes all the way to the skin.

IF YOUR PUP IS NERVOUS, keep talking gently and soothingly throughout the whole bath. Lather the coat up thoroughly, using massage motions with your hands. Not only does this make sure the shampoo gets right into the skin, but it can also help to calm the puppy.

. . .

RINSE THOROUGHLY, ensuring no traces of shampoo are left. Towel-dry your puppy before he gets the chance to shake himself dry, or you will be cleaning more than the puppy!

KEEP him in a warm room until he dries out properly. Give him a brush afterward to remove any dead or loose hairs.

Nail Care

A puppy's nails will overgrow, and they will need trimming regularly. You can use an ordinary nail clipper or a proper dog clipper for this. Many people take their dog or puppy to a specialist to trim nails.

START EARLY. Get your puppy used to you handling his feet and reward with treats. Leave the clippers where the puppy can see them and get used to them.

SIT the puppy on your lap and make sure your trimmers are sharp. Hold the puppy's foot firmly and push the pads to make the nail protrude. Examine the nail to see where the quick finishes and clip off at a 45-degree angle. If the puppy has dark nails, do this gradually because it won't be easy to see the quick ends.

NEVER CUT the quick (this is the pink section) because it will hurt and bleed. Don't forget to trim the dewclaws on either side of the leg. If they are left, they can grow long and curl into the leg, causing a lot of pain and expense having them removed.

TRIM ONCE EVERY TWO WEEKS, and make sure you praise your puppy and reward him after every session. Don't worry if things don't go to plan the first time around; it may take a while for your puppy to get used to it.

Dental Care

As a puppy grows, so do his teeth, and they need to look after properly. If you plan to brush your pup's teeth, make sure you do it regularly and start him young so he can get used to it.

Sit the puppy on your lap and lift his lips on either side of the mouth. Talk soothingly to him and give him a reward when he lets you do it without fuss.

Next, start by rubbing your fingers over his teeth gently. Wrap a washcloth around your fingers to do this. You only need to worry about the front surface of the teeth on a dog. Once your puppy has gotten used to that, move to a soft toothbrush; a baby's toothbrush is ideal. Soak the brush in warm water and gently brush his teeth. Once he is used to that, move on to toothpaste. You need to use a specially formulated one for this, as dogs don't tend to like the taste of human toothpaste.

If you don't feel comfortable brushing your puppy's teeth, there is a wide range of dental chews that you can buy at a reasonable price. These are designed to do the same thing—remove plaque from the teeth.

At the age of about five months, your puppy will begin to lose his milk teeth, and permanent teeth will take their place. Ensure he has a good choice of chew toys because he will be in some pain while teething and will want to chew anything and everything.

. . .

CHECK his teeth and around his mouth every week. He should have white teeth and pink gums. If his adult teeth start to grow before his milk teeth fall out, you will need to take him to a vet.

Professional Groomers

If you have a long-haired breed, it is a great idea to take your puppy to a professional groomer at least twice a year. They are experienced professionals who can do anything to groom and keep your dog in the best possible hygiene.

How to Handle Hot Weather

Summertime can be tough on dogs. Make sure that your pup stays hydrated all of the time and give it plenty of shade. You also need to make sure that your puppy gets enough exercise, but you probably need to make some adjustments to ensure that your dog adapts to the weather. Whenever you're outside, always make sure to bring extra bottles of water for your dog.

NEVER LEAVE your puppy inside the car by itself. Having your pup inside the car with the windows closed during the summertime can be dangerous for your dog.

TEMPERATURES TEND TO FLUCTUATE WILDLY, and dogs can get very dehydrated. Your dog can suffer from severe brain damage, or worse, it can die.

EVEN LEAVING the windows open by a few inches won't help your pup. Always make sure that your dog stays indoors during the warmest times of the day. Don't shave its fur completely, however, as it can protect your dog from sunburns.

If possible, you might want to bring some sunscreen with you. You can ask your veterinarian for recommendations.

9

HEALTH CARE FOR PUPPIES

Remember that your dog entirely depends on you for its health, safety, and grooming. Spend time caring for your dog because this creates a bond between the two of you.

The American Veterinary Medical Association recommends giving your dog a balanced diet, enough exercise, and regular checkups as well as neutering to keep it free from parasites.

Your veterinarian knows a lot about your dog's health, so make sure to find one you can trust.

Vet Visit

When you bring your puppy home, let him settle in for a day or two and then take him to the veterinarian for a health check. If you bought your puppy from a shelter, you could check with the shelter, as they may be able to give you a discount.

. . .

Make sure you tell the veterinarian it is a new puppy, and they will allocate you more time to do a thorough check. When you are at the vet, keep your puppy with you and do not let him come into contact with other dogs. They may have a disease that he will catch easily since his immune system is not fully developed at this stage.

The veterinarian will:

- Give your pup a thorough check-up.
- Talk to you about vaccinations (let them know of any that he has had already). You should have certificates for all previous vaccinations.
- Talk to you about microchips and worming and flea treatment programs.
- Discuss neutering or spaying with you for when the puppy is old enough.
- Answer your questions about general health care, feeding, and exercising.
- Give you details of training classes you can attend.

Weekly Checklist

Illnesses and other problems can be detrimental to the growth and development of a puppy. Once a week:

- Check his ears. Do they look clean and smell fresh? If his ears are dirty or smell bad, have red patches on them, or if your pup continually shakes his head, see a veterinarian. It could indicate infection, ear mites, or some other more serious problem.
- Get close up and smell his breath! If it smells terrible, he either has problems with his teeth and mouth or an upset stomach.
- Stroke your puppy all over, feeling lumps, scratches,

and bumps. Run your hands against his coat so that his hair stands on end. Examine the skin and hair roots for parasites or tiny black specks, which indicate fleas.
- Check his eyes and nose for discharge.
- Check under the tail; his rear should be clean. If there is any dirt, signs of worms, or red sore patches, again, contact your veterinarian. If your puppy continually scrapes his bottom on the ground, that is a good indication of the presence of worms.

Signs of Illness

As we all know, prevention is far better than a cure, and it is never truer than with a puppy. Provided you have created a safe environment, feed him a balanced diet, and exercise him properly, your puppy will thrive.

Sometimes, though, illnesses happen. But, if you have been doing your weekly health checks, you will know your puppy very well and spot the signs of anything amiss early enough to do something about it. The following are signs that something may be wrong if your puppy:

- He loses his appetite for more than a day
- Suddenly becomes uncontrollably hungry
- Drinks more than normal
- Is lethargic
- He shakes his head or continuously scratches
- Changes in character noticeably
- Develops lumps, bumps, or cuts
- Has a discharge coming from his eyes or nose
- Moves differently (i.e., limps, turns in circles, holds his head over to one side)

- Has severe diarrhea that goes on for more than twenty-four hours
- He is constipated or has signs of blood or worms in his feces

You should notify your veterinarian immediately if any of these are occurring. It's cheaper and easier to treat an illness or condition if it is caught early. Do consider your insurance as well, but be aware that there will be a limit on the number of claims you can make.

Vaccinations

The following vaccinations are essential, as they can prevent some truly life-threatening diseases:

- Parvovirus
- Distemper
- Hepatitis
- Parainfluenza
- Leptospirosis

Flea Treatment

All dogs will get fleas unless they are prevented. The main reason for flea treatment is to stop your puppy from becoming infested. Signs of fleas include a very irritable and restless puppy, scratching constantly, and biting himself. In addition, you may notice black dots when you comb your puppy. These are specks of dried blood and are a definitive sign that your puppy has fleas.

Seek advice from your veterinarian about flea control. Make sure you wash all of his bedding thoroughly and then spray it or sprinkle flea powder on it. You will also need to spray or powder anywhere in the house where the puppy has been.

WORMING

Puppies, in particular, are prone to worms and can get roundworm, hookworm, tapeworm, or whipworm. Your veterinarian can give you a general wormer to work with or give you specific tablets for specific worms.

ROUNDWORMS ARE USUALLY PASSED from the mother to the puppy through the milk (if Mommy hasn't been adequately wormed) and can cause diseases, stunt growth, and slow down development. They cause a rounded potbelly and diarrhea in a puppy and are also known as zoonotic, which means that they can spread to you, and the larvae can cause you serious problems. If you see worms in the puppy's stool, make sure your puppy is wormed to schedule.

Neutering or Spaying

If you adopt a puppy from a shelter, neutering or spaying may already have been done depending on their age. If they are too young, discuss with your veterinarian and see if the shelter or breeder can get you a discount on the operation. Reasons for having your puppy neutered or spayed are:

FEMALES:

- Preventing them from having seasons, thus stopping any chance of pregnancy and all sorts of dogs hanging around
- Prevention of breast cancer
- Prevention of ovarian cancer
- Prevention of uterine cancer or disease

Males:

- Undesirable behavior when females are in heat
- Prevention of testicular cancer
- Prevention of hormonal diseases

Spaying or neutering also calms a dog down, although, afterward, especially with females, you will need to watch their diet, as they will be more likely to put on weight.

Exercising your Puppy

Having a puppy is great. But, because you have to exercise regularly, you will benefit as well! Keeping fit is extremely important for a puppy to keep his weight down, build up his muscles, and develop a strong cardiovascular system and immune system.

HOWEVER, avoid over-exercising your puppy. Bear in mind that his bones and muscles are still developing and can be easily injured. Instead, play in the garden to start with, and then, when he has had all his vaccinations, you can start to take him for short walks.

10

PUPPY TRAINING MISTAKES

Getting a new puppy is exciting. If you don't know the basic "do's" and "don'ts" of training your puppy, things can take a turn for the worse very quickly. You are doing the right things since you are trying to train your puppy. Potty training problems, constantly chewing on everything, incessant barking, and other "bad" behaviors could change all those great feelings into regret and frustration. Don't allow a minor mistake to get in your way. Although they are insignificant, it might surprise you to learn that some things could slow down your training progress. If you can stay away from these common mistakes, you will increase your chances of enjoying your new puppy and mentoring them into adulthood.

Here are some mistakes you need to stay away from:

Taking Them From Mom Too Soon

This is probably the biggest mistake people make. In the first eight weeks of a dog's life, they are getting lots of nurturing from mom, and they are learning valuable social skills from their siblings.

Unfortunately, some shelters and breeders take the puppies away from their mom and siblings way too soon. It cuts short the social imprinting process, and it could cause some problems. For example, if the puppy leaves the litter too soon, they usually have issues learning not to bite, and they won't know how to interact the right way with people and other dogs. They could also get skittish toward people they don't know and other animals. Stay away from these problems that can last their entire life by just waiting until your puppy is older than eight weeks to take them away from their siblings and mom.

Waiting Too Long

You need to start training your puppy the minute you get them home. It doesn't matter how old they are either. Don't try to wait until they get a bit older because, by this time, they have probably begun developing bad habits. Training your dog isn't the same as "behavior management." With training, your goal is to shape the puppy's behavior to teach them ways to respond to specific phrases.

Puppies that are too young may not be ready to learn some advanced commands, but you still need to begin working on basic commands and house training. With time, you are going to create deeper bonds with your dog. They are going to get accustomed to your routines as they mature. You can then try some more fun things such as tricks. You can then try some advanced training or tricks.

You Run Back Inside After The Puppy Pees or Poops

Puppies love being outside and want to explore their area; it isn't going to take them long to learn that all their fun is over after pee or poop. Because of this, you might have a dog who will not go to the bathroom outside until they can't hold it anymore. It could cause problems when you are in a hurry, and you need them to go potty fast. What you need to be doing is taking your puppy outside on a leash while waiting patiently until they have done their business. When they have finished, give them praise and a reward and then take them for a short walk or play with them for a bit. By doing this, they will learn how to potty and will go as soon as you take them outside.

Allowing Your Dog To Give "Love Nibbles"

Puppies are going to use their teeth to explore just like a toddler will use their hands. You can expect them to put their mouth and teeth on everything anytime they get excited. Allowing them to give you nips when playing with them might seem harmless, but this isn't something you want your dog to do once they are grown. If you have already let your puppy do this, you can redirect them to a toy when they begin biting you. When they tug on the suitable toy, give them praise and reward them by playing with them. Puppies grow extremely fast, so play as much as you can with them.

Not Crate Training Them

Dogs are naturally denning animals, and they love having snug spots where they can nest or eat. Crates take advantage of their natural desire to not soil where they eat or sleep. A crate is the best place to feed your puppy because they will be able to eat by themselves away from people or other pets you might have. Choose a crate that is appropriate for your breed of dog. It needs to be tall enough so your puppy can stand up in it and long enough so they can turn around inside. If the crate is too big, they might use the bathroom in one part of it and sleep in the other. Feed them inside the crate and get them to sleep in it, too. If you can't be with them all the time, they need to be in their crate or have a puppy sitter. Even though they can sleep in the crate during the night, it is best not to make them stay in the crate no more than six hours overnight or four hours in the daytime.

. . .

Using a "One-Size-Fits-All" Training

Don't get the first dog training book you see; read it, and think that is all you have to do. Don't just talk to one friend who has dogs, either. There are several successful programs and styles of dog training, and there won't be two dogs who are the same. Sometimes you might need to talk to several people and use all the information you have collected to create a training program that works for you and your dog.

Try out different things and see which ones work the best for your dog. Combine various types of training to make a plan that will fit your dog and you. You could even try some different training classes. Never give up too fast, but never be afraid to change if things aren't working out for you.

You Get Too Excited When Your Doorbell Rings

It is great to share the excitement of having a pizza delivered or friends coming to your house. However, you are psyching up your puppy when you rush to the door, or you ask them: "Who's at the door?" This could cause bad habits such as jumping on guests, running to the door, or your puppy running out the door and into the streets. Keep your greeting low-key from the start and train your puppy to be nice when you have visitors. You could put them on a leash if you know you have people over and give them praise and rewards when they stay at your side without jumping on others. You could train them to get in their crate when the doorbell rings and then give them praise and a treat for staying there until you call them.

Letting Them Be Too Independent

Puppies are going to be curious about their surroundings. If you let your puppy wander around your home without supervision, they are going to get into some kind of trouble. For example, they could begin chewing on shoes, clothing, loose wires, going potty inside, or finding a way to get outside and possibly getting hurt. Most "accidents" that happen in the home are caused by not being supervised well and will cause delays in getting them house-trained. You can prevent this by ensuring that your new puppy is in their crate, with you, or inside a fenced-in yard. When they are inside, you can try keeping their leash tethered to your belt so they can go with you when inside. This shows them where they are allowed to go. Once their house training is done and they don't have any more accidents, you can slowly start increasing their independence when inside.

Being Inconsistent

You have to keep your responses to your dog consistent when you are training them. If you don't, you are only confusing your puppy. In addition, you might find that you have accidentally reinforced some bad behaviors.

Look at this example: you have made a rule that the puppy can't get on the couch. You are feeling down one day and want to have some cuddle time with them. You let them get on the couch with you to help you feel better. The next day you fuss at them for jumping up on the sofa; they aren't going to understand why they can't be with you today but got to cuddle with you yesterday.

Begging would be another example of this kind of mistake. If you never give your puppy any of the food you are eating, they will not get into the habit of begging for food when you eat. They might try it a couple of times, but ignoring them or telling them to lay down will discourage this behavior. If somebody gives him some food, they will associate begging with a reward and continue to beg.

. . .

One more example would be rewarding your dog any time they "sort of" do a command right. For example, if you are trying to train your puppy to lie down, you only give them a reward when their entire body is on the floor. If you were to provide them with a reward BEFORE their entire body is down, this is inconsistent. When you tell them to "lie down," they might get confused and keep doing it wrong.

Pulling While Leash Training

Puppies are going to do what will work for them. If you let your puppy pull when you are leash training them, they are going to do it forever, even when they are a BIG dog. Going for walks with your puppy isn't going to be any fun, plus you might be hurting your back and shoulders in the process. Teach your puppy from the beginning that keeping their leash loose will get them praise, treats, and fun walks. Anytime the pulling begins, stop walking. When you stay consistent, they will learn the correct way to walk rather than be a bulldozer and pull you forward.

Keeping Food Out At All Times

Leaving food out all day is a huge mistake. When you let them eat all day long, you are lessening your chances of creating a potty schedule. If they always have food in their belly, they will need to go to the potty more often. When you feed them at a certain time each day, you will be "synchronizing" their system. This is going to make house-training them easier, too. Feeding at certain times will create a better food drive with your puppy. Being able to predict when they are hungry is an excellent training tool. About 20 minutes before their meal, they are going to do anything for a treat. Feeding at specific times will let you know precisely the amount of food they are eating. By doing this, you will be able to keep them at a perfect weight. People who freely feed their puppies don't know exactly how much food they are eating because you add to their dish during the day.

Harsh Discipline

Most dog trainers today will agree that punishing your puppy during training is not effective at all. Dogs will perform better for a reward through positivity. Using mild aversions like shaking a rattle can or spray bottle of water could help you in certain situations and don't cause the puppy any harm. However, other things might cause a dangerous problem. Harsh discipline is any actions like jerking their leash, grabbing them by the scruff of their neck, staring them down, alpha rolls, hitting them, or yelling at them. Every one of these actions has bad consequences like:

1. Provoking aggressive reaction from your puppy that puts you or others in danger
2. It could make your dog scared of you
3. You might hurt your puppy

If you think that harsh discipline is needed to become dominant to your dog, you are doing everything wrong. Considering that humans are "pack leaders" is a very outdated concept and comes from inaccurate research about wolves and dogs. You need to do some research and learn ways you can earn your dog's respect. Their training process needs to be fun for them and you. It is an excellent way for you to create a closer bond with your dog. It should never be about bullying them into submission.

Rubbing Their Nose In Their Accidents

A puppy who is only ten weeks old doesn't know what you are teaching her when you shove their nose into their poop. The only thing you are showing them is that you get mad when they poop. This only teaches them to be scared of their poop. This could make them poop in spots where you can't see it like in a closet or behind furniture. If you crate train them the right way, you will not have this problem. If you catch them pooping inside, clap a few times and say "aah-ahh" and get them outside as fast as you can. When they do go outside, remember to reward them. If they did poop inside, make sure you clean it well with an enzyme cleaner.

CONCLUSION

Thanks for reading through the book. I hope that you have found everything informative and helpful. Welcoming a new puppy into your life can be a wonderful and exciting experience. However, it can get overwhelming with the number of things you need to do.

If this is your first time adding a puppy to your family, you might feel overwhelmed by your decisions, but what it all boils down to is everyone just wants a great pet. So I have started you off on a path of research and findings that will help you and your puppy reach that brass ring.

Ideally, you want to make the best breed choice when picking your new family member, but we all know that sometimes a dog will choose you. To help you make the best decisions, I have tried to prepare helpful information to help you narrow down your search, discuss options with breeders, and prepare your home before your puppy arrives.

I know how hard it can be to choose a new food for your puppy. Therefore, I have provided up-to-date nutritional information along with health and wellness advice concerning any vaccination schedules you need to be aware of.

Every puppy needs to learn the basics, and, with my instructions, you will be able to teach your puppy essential life lessons such as crate training, potty training, leash training, and basic commands. I have also gone into great detail about furthering your training options and building upon learned skills. Within these disciplines, you and your canine companion may find a future calling and develop a bond to last your lifetime together.

Socialization for your puppy is an important step and can head off other problems that may surface down the road. Unfortunately, many owners do not realize how vital socialization is when impacting further education.

With this book, you should have the information you need to help get your puppy established in their new home, housebroken, and happy. Puppies are a big ball of fun, so you can't expect all of this to work overnight. Give them time, and give yourself time. If something doesn't seem to be working just right, try doing it a different way. Eventually, everything will come together. You will find that you can read your dog without any problems, and you won't be cleaning up pee out of the floor forever.

I wish you and any future puppy that comes into your life the best experiences possible and hope you have many beautiful hours of playtime together. To experience the love of a dog is like no other attachment. They give us everything they have, and all they want is our affection. From Hollywood to service dogs, they bring us their unique love, intelligence, and devotion.

I sincerely thank you for purchasing this book, and I hope that you now feel more confident and prepared to welcome your newfound companion into your family. Please take a minute and leave a quick review of this book. Your review would mean the world to me.

Good luck!

www.ingramcontent.com/pod-product-compliance
Ingram Content Group UK Ltd.
Pitfield, Milton Keynes, MK11 3LW, UK
UKHW020423250726
13967UKWH00007B/2783

9 781954 937192